BAKED

NEW FRONTIERS IN BAKING

BY MATT LEWIS AND RENATO POLIAFITO

PHOTOGRAPHS BY TINA RUPP

STEWART, TABORI & CHANG

NEW YORK

CONTENTS

ACKNOWLEDGMENTS

Running a bakery is demanding, and writing a book is difficult, but writing a book while running a bakery is insane. Thankfully, we had a small cadre of friends, acquaintances, and associates to help us along. We are forever grateful.

First and foremost, a big round of love to Alison Fargis at Stonesong. She is a wickedly funny friend and a superb agent, and we are so thrilled that she saw the possibilities for a Baked book many moons ago.

Another big round of thanks goes to Luisa Weiss and the entire Stewart, Tabori and Chang team. Luisa was kind and very, very patient with our haphazard schedules and slight A.D.D. Luisa is a shrewd editor and a fantastic recipe tester, and we could not have shaped this book without her. Thanks also to Alissa Faden for designing a book that embodies the Baked philosophy.

Laura Lehrman and Andrea Chin deserve special recognition for pushing the Baked lifestyle on the masses. They have been working with us since before we opened and they were always believers.

Tina Rupp is a dreamy food photographer and a saint. We decided to shoot the book without all the hoopla of a dedicated food stylist (to keep it real) and she was completely on board. Both Leslie Seigel, the prop stylist, and Teresa Horgan, the photo assistant, were huge assets during the frantic photography sessions.

Christina Vann is an illustrator extraordinaire who added just the right amount of whimsy to this book.

The backbone of Baked is our staff. Baking is in their blood and their talents are extreme. Some employees have been with us for many years and some just passed through, but we owe them all a big round of thanks.

Blair Van Sant, Eric Wolitzky, Jessica Bacchus, and Ryan Ermold are expert pastry chefs and they have elevated the Baked kitchen to new heights. Additionally, they each performed many duties on this book, from styling the shots to adapting the recipes.

Finally, we owe a great debt to the folks that keep Baked running smoothly on a daily basis. Janet "Suki" Olguin is a stern taskmaster who keeps the whole show running; Agatha Vassallo can ice twenty cakes in the time it takes to pour a cup of coffee; Stefania Rubicondo keeps the gears going; Jessie Sheehan makes a mean batch of granola; and Liz, Joe, Pascual, Monica, Emma, and Rafi all make Baked possible in so many ways.

We have to thank our persistent recipe testers, who tested when we just couldn't look at another cake or brownie. Sarah Copeland gave levelheaded advice, Joann Tamburro provided all manner of perspective (and photos), Elizabeth Moore somehow tested between her two jobs, and Nick Martin and Reid Thompson gave some of our slightly daunting recipes a try.

Special thanks to Leslie Heffler-Flick and Kristine Moberg for giving so much to a start-up bakery.

And thank you to Jacques Torres for all of his kind help, and Martha Stewart for giving Baked a big platform.

Matt would like to thank his dad, Larry, for being a sounding board and recipe tester; Matt Holbein for all the right reasons; and Gretchen, Nancy, Ann Boreali, Brad, and Steph "Copper Pot."

Renato would like to thank his mom, dad, his sister Marisa and brother Nino for having faith in him; Sven and Tina, for being so nice to come home to; and Anne, Aaron, Michelle, Rocky, Stephen, and Sean for being great recipe testers and, more importantly, great friends.

This book is dedicated to our moms. They are the sweetest.

INTRODUCTION

GETTING BAKED

THE IDEA

Baked, the coffee shop and the bakery, opened its doors on January 11, 2005, in the vast industrialized section of Brooklyn called Red Hook. However, long before Baked opened and long before we even had an oven or a mixer in place, we had an idea.

The idea was both simple and daunting. We wanted to create "the" classic American bakery in a city swarming with hundreds of delicious bakeries, and we wanted Baked to be the best in its niche. We wanted to serve the best coffee with the best slice of cake and have it served by a well-informed counter person with a warm smile (if you are not already aware, New York City counter people are not big on "warm smiles").

We set about testing cakes and cookies and scones in various home kitchens while the bakery was being pieced together in Red Hook. We gained a few pounds (all in the service of bettering humankind), and honed our baking philosophy. We would reduce sugar where possible, increase the amounts of chocolate where possible (there is no such thing as too much chocolate), and incorporate as many local and seasonal ingredients as feasible.

At the end of our testing phase we had our dream menu. Fluffy cakes covered in cooked frostings. Crisp, chewy cookies. Dark, fudgelike brownies. Tall scones, candylike tarts, and the best marshmallows ever. More than a few items included the perfect combination of peanut butter and chocolate, and even more of our desserts featured our favorite flavor, malt.

CONSTRUCTION

We were ready. The store wasn't.

Converting our space to a bakery from the remains of a storefront church was tragicomical. The existing plumbing was almost nonfunctional. The floors would not support equipment, people, or, in some places, a large cupcake. The electrical system could barely power an electric tea kettle and a hot plate.

As the construction dragged on, we rented a small commercial kitchen (and we mean really small) and fulfilled a few holiday orders in hopes of defraying some of our costly delays. During the days, we would bake large amounts of brownies and blondies and during the nights we would sit at home and wrap and box the orders on Matt's dining table. These were very long days and nights.

We had a great construction crew and a talented design firm, but we still suffered many months of delays, sleepless nights, and dwindling bank accounts. We swore to each other that any future spaces would be built in very new, very well constructed buildings. The charm and allure of an old space in an old building didn't seem worth all the stress and anxiety.

OPENING

Our grand opening, in the dead of a New York winter, was a blur of cakes, hot chocolate, smooth music, kudos, and happy people. We were exhausted, but cheerful and content. Our bakery seemed to please both the pastry enthusiast and the casual cupcake customer alike. Most important, we started to see an influx of repeat customers (always a good sign for our type of business).

Over the next few months, we started increasing the yields on our recipes to meet the demand. In January 2005 we were making forty-eight cookies per day, by June we were making two hundred, and the numbers have been increasing ever since. Our cakes and brownies have followed the same trajectory.

We also started adding new items to our repertoire. Some, like the celebrated Sweet and Salty Cake, were the result of a combination of customer suggestion and kitchen intuition. Others, like the well-loved but complex Icebox Tower Cake, were created by committee in the kitchen to fill a nostalgic need and evolved into beautiful and stunning desserts.

Eventually, our bakery started to win awards and appear in the editorial pages of both food and nonfood magazines. We even began to appear on a few TV shows to spread the gospel of Baked. The attention from the awards and the press and the TV appearances was greatly appreciated, and sometimes overwhelming.

Six months after we opened, and long before we had all of our systems in place, we were awarded a prime position in Oprah's magazine, O. Our brownies were one of her favorite things. (Thanks, Oprah.) The full-page brownie photo was centerfold worthy: big, gorgeous, glossy, and seductive. Moments after the magazine hit newsstands, the phone started ringing incessantly and orders started piling up on the Internet. We were ecstatic, but neither of us could foresee any feasible way of fulfilling the orders. We called in every talented baker, boxer, wrapper, and friend we knew to help us through

the madness. We made it—a bit battle scarred, but we made it. Everyone who ordered brownies received brownies, and we learned a lot in the process.

One year later, we made our Sweet and Salty Cake on the *Martha Stewart Show*, and moments after the show aired people were ordering the cake for every conceivable celebration and occasion. To this day, it's our best-selling cake, and we have Martha Stewart to thank. (Thanks, Martha.)

NOW

Baked is still here, and we are still busy. Somehow, the place just feels warmer and more inviting with each passing month. The floors are a bit more worn, and the paint isn't quite as shiny as when we opened, but it really feels like an integral part of the neighborhood now. Like it's been here forever.

The neighborhood has changed slightly (like all of New York City has changed slightly), but the locals and regulars who stop by are still the best locals and regulars a small business could hope for.

OUR BOOK

The greatest compliment a neighborhood bakery can receive from a customer is a request for a recipe. It means we've become a part of people's lives, their friends. It isn't unusual for us to hear, "This is fantastic. Can I have the recipe?" or "Is this cake easy to make? I want to make one for my grandmother's birthday." We've always done our best to provide recipes to those who asked, but most of them had not been written with the home baker in mind. (Unless, of course, the home baker was interested in making 12 cakes at a time or 128 marshmallows or 16 loaves of quickbread.)

The recipes in this book are for you. It is our collection of greatest hits, customer favorites, and a few of our own obscure obsessions. We tested and ate and tested and ate every recipe over and over to ensure that they would be just as good in your kitchen as they are in ours.

We wish you many happy baking occasions.

Many cheers,
Matt and Renato

1

A FIELD
GUIDE TO BAKING

The varied recipes in this book run the gamut from our customers' favorite biscuits to our award-winning cakes to our favorite boozy after-dinner drinks. In writing each recipe, it was our goal to make baking fun and approachable for everyone. We distilled our many years of dessert experience into each recipe, and we look forward to sharing them with you.

This chapter expands on some of the baking tools, terms, techniques, and tips we mention in the recipes in the following chapters.

TOOLS AND EQUIPMENT

You need only a few basic tools to produce every baked good in this book (and most baked goods in general). Here they are:

BAKING SHEETS: We recommend using heavy-duty, inexpensive, light-colored, rimmed baking sheets. We almost always bake on heavy aluminum half sheet pans (18 by 13 inches) at home, and you can pick these up at a restaurant supply retailer. Do not waste your money on the supposedly scientifically calibrated insulated cookie sheets or those with the nonstick coatings. They are worthless. Make sure you have a roll of parchment paper in your baking supplies to line your baking sheets.

BLENDER: A blender is a handy, though not necessary, tool to have around the kitchen. We use a blender to mix smoothies, shakes, and ice cream bases. Though not always an ideal substitution, a food processor can handle most of these tasks just as well.

BROWNIE AND BAR PANS: Most of the bar cookie recipes in this book are designed for a standard 9-by-13-inch light metal or glass baking pan. Why such a big pan? It's party-sized, providing almost twenty-four servings. And if you're not throwing a party, give the extras to neighbors or coworkers, or stash them in the freezer for later. Avoid dark-colored pans, as they will create unsavory, well-done crisp edges.

BUNDT PAN: Every baker should have at least one bundt pan in his baking collection. We use the basic 10- and 12-cup versions made by Nordic Ware. They're heavy, easy to use, and should last forever. There are also many decorative bundt pans on the market (rosettes, castles), and you can absolutely use them for our bundt recipes. Just make sure to grease all the nooks and crannies of the specialty pans so the cake comes out cleanly.

CAKE PANS: Keep it simple, straightforward, and economical. We suggest using professional aluminum cake pans, available from almost any kitchen supply store. Stay away from dark pans to prevent crisp cake edges.

CAKE TURNTABLE: It is much easier to decorate a cake (or sugar cookies or brownies) on a cake turntable. Just set the cake on the stand and turn as you frost and decorate. Cake turntables can be found at almost any kitchen supply store.

CANDY AND CHOCOLATE THERMOMETERS: For the beginning candy maker, we recommend an old-school and inexpensive clip-on candy thermometer. It should have gradations of 2 to 5 degrees and have a range of 100 to 400 degrees F. Also, many basic candy thermometers mark all the stages of candy making (hard ball, soft ball, and so on), making life even easier. This type of thermometer should cost no more than $15.

Chocolate thermometers are completely different. They all have 1-degree gradations (for accurate tempering) and they do not read above 130 degrees F. There is only one recipe in this book that requires tempering, though you might want to purchase a cheap chocolate thermometer (about $15) for other uses.

COOLING RACKS: One Christmas, Matt's mother gave him a cooling rack that was large enough to hold a small car. With no place in the kitchen to store it, he exchanged it for three small racks. With cooling racks, smaller is better. Look for ones that will fit perfectly over a half sheet pan so you can use one to easily coat an item in ganache.

DOUBLE BOILER: A double boiler is a great way to melt chocolate or chocolate and butter together or to warm egg whites. To concoct a double boiler, you need one medium-sized saucepan filled with water and one (preferably metal) bowl that sits partway inside the pan without touching the water.

FOOD PROCESSOR: We promise you will not regret owning a large food processor. We know they are oversized, heavy, not exactly beautiful, and often viewed as difficult to clean. However, once you've owned a food processor, you will never give it up. It chops nuts and graham crackers with ease. It makes batters, icing, and pie dough with the flick of a switch. It's like an assistant, only better. Go get one. It has many uses in the savory kitchen as well.

ICE CREAM MAKER: Ice cream makers are fun to have around and experiment with. We both own the same $50 Cuisinart ice cream machine and it works just fine (as long as you freeze the bowl ahead of time). For the more serious ice cream maker, there are more serious machines with larger capacities and built-in compressors that eliminate the whole frozen-bowl business.

ICE CREAM SCOOP: We use several different-sized ice cream scoops with a release mechanism to measure cookie doughs and portion cake batters (not to mention scooping ice cream).

MEASURING CUPS AND SPOONS: For liquid measurements we recommend Pyrex (glass) 2-cup and 4-cup measures. They also come in very handy for melting butter in a microwave oven.

For dry measurements, we recommend a basic set of metal measuring cups from ¼ cup to 2 cups.

We measure dry ingredients by scooping into the cup from another larger cup, then leveling to the top of the cup. All light and dark brown sugars should be packed tightly, leveled to the top of the cup.

For measuring spoons, just use the most basic set of metal spoons you can find. They usually come locked together by a metal ring and start with ¼ teaspoon and go up to 1 tablespoon. Measure all ingredients level with the rim of the spoon.

MICROPLANE: The term *microplane* has become synonymous with the long and thin graters found in commercial and home kitchens. At home, we use one grater strictly for spices and one grater strictly for zesting fruit. At one time, Matt owned both a Microplane and a ridiculous tool specifically for zesting. He donated the zester to a friend and has never needed it since.

MICROWAVE OVEN: If you have a microwave, great. One short burst of low power, and butter and chocolate are melted. If you don't have a microwave, no worries: You can melt butter and chocolate using the double boiler method (page 23).

MIXING BOWLS: You should own one set of melamine mixing bowls, and they should nest, and they should have a small spout for easy pouring. Melamine bowls are lightweight, super cheap, and easy to clean. We forgive you for insisting on using your favorite heavy ceramic bowls. (For reasons unknown, Renato has still not given up on using the Fire King jadite mixing bowl he found on eBay.) We know they are beautiful and perhaps antique or family heirlooms, but they are just not as easy to maneuver as the lightweight melamine.

OFFSET SPATULA: We use a small, metal offset spatula for small, detail-oriented jobs like smoothing cake batters while in the pan, loosening cakes from the sides of pans, removing the first brownie, and swirling or marbling batters.

PARCHMENT PAPER: We use parchment a lot to line cookie sheets, cake pans, and the like. Parchment keeps items from sticking to the pan, and it is much less messy than greasing the pans or spraying them with cooking spray. You can't use parchment for everything (not than we didn't try), but it's the best option most of the time. By the by, when baking cookies in batches, you can use the same parchment multiple times.

PIE PLATE OR TIN: You can bake a pie in almost any pie plate or tin. We like ceramic plates, aluminum tins, and, for some occasions, a Pyrex (glass) plate. They all work equally well, though we love the look of a pie baked in a unique ceramic plate.

PIE WEIGHTS: When prebaking the shell for a single-crust pie, weights serve to help the dough keep its shape. You can buy specialty pie weights from most kitchen stores or make your own (see page 95).

STAND MIXER: Every home baker or baking enthusiast should have a standing mixer with at least three basic attachments: a whisk, a paddle, and a dough hook. Though big and a bit expensive, a standing mixer is an essential item. Matt has had his Kitchen Aid stand mixer for eleven years, and it still works as well as the first day he plugged it in.

SPATULA: You will use a spatula in almost every recipe in this book. Our advice is to buy an assortment of three or four silicone spatulas in different sizes, and use them for scraping down bowls, mixing light batters, and folding in egg whites or flour.

SPRINGFORM PAN: We use a basic light-colored 9-inch springform pan for the Upstate Cheesecake (page 85) and the Flourless Chocolate Cake (page 50). Unless you have dreams of starting a cheesecake business out of your home, we think you only need one of these pans in your home equipment collection.

TART PANS: We have an assortment of large and small tart pans floating around the bakery and at home. We use both a 9-inch removable-bottom tart pan (which makes it easier to dislodge the tart) and a 4-inch minitart pan in this book. When storing minitart pans, we suggest layering them between sheets of paper towels or parchment paper to make sure they do not become stuck when nesting.

WHISK: Home bakers should not worry about owning the many varied types of whisks on the market. We use a very basic wire whisk with a sturdy wooden handle (medium to large will do) for every recipe that calls for a whisk in this book. Whisks are great tools for combining dry ingredients (whisking flour, baking soda, and salt together, for instance), but do not use your whisk as an everyday stirring device (a silicone spatula works better), as you can whisk too much air into your batters accidentally.

TERMS, TECHNIQUES, AND TIPS

CHOCOLATE: It is imperative when making a chocolate dessert to use the best possible chocolate. Luckily, many great brands are available at the local supermarket. We tested the recipes in this book using Callebaut and Scharffen Berger, and we highly recommend both.

CHOCOLATE PERCENTAGES: The percentage label on a bar of chocolate is confusing. For instance, one brand's 64% chocolate bar is often completely different from another brand's 64% chocolate bar. The percentage refers to the cocoa mass in the bar itself. While we could write an entire chapter on this subject, we recommend the following bars for this book's recipes:

If a recipe calls for a dark chocolate with 60 to 72% cocoa content, use any of the following:

Scharffen Berger's Home Baking Bar 62% (found in most supermarkets)

Scharffen Berger's Home Baking Bar 70% (found in most supermarkets)

Callebaut Chocolate Block 60% (found in specialty markets—often chopped and repackaged by the specialty market)

Callebaut Chocolate Block 70% (found in specialty markets—often chopped and repackaged by the specialty market)

If a recipe calls for a milk chocolate, use either of the following:

Jacques Torres Milk Chocolate Bar (found in specialty markets and online)

Scharffen Berger Milk Chocolate Bar 41% (found in most supermarkets)

Of course, there are many other wonderful brands of chocolate you can use, and as you get more familiar with the different brands, you will start to align yourself with a few favorites. See Sources (page 198) for a list of where to buy fine baking chocolates.

COCOA POWDER: We made every recipe in this book with Valrhona unsweetened cocoa powder. It is deep, dark, and delicious. Don't get too caught up in the Dutched (cocoa powder treated with alkali) versus natural cocoa debate. Instead, pay more attention to the color and smell of the cocoa powder you are using. Some mass-produced cocoas are almost gray in color. Avoid them. If you can't find Valrhona, look for a dark-colored cocoa. We never use sweetened cocoa in this book (or, for that matter, at all).

CRUMB COAT: Essentially, a crumb coat is a very thin layer of frosting applied to the cake to keep the light crumbs suspended so they won't appear in the final layer of frosting. It's like the first coat of paint; it lays the foundation for the next and final coat. A crumb-coated cake should be refrigerated for at least 15 minutes prior to applying the next frosting layer.

FOLDING: Folding is the act of gently (no fast stirring, no whisking) putting two parts of a batter together. The best way to fold something together is to use a rubber or silicone spatula and fold the bottom part of the batter (often the heavier part) into the top part of the batter (often the lighter part): Cut down through the two layers in the center of the bowl, then sweep the spatula along the bottom of the bowl toward you and lift the spatula up and over again to the center; turn the bowl 90 degrees and repeat until the batter is just combined.

GELATIN SHEETS: We use gelatin sheets to make the most light and fluffy marshmallows. Gelatin sheets are readily available at most specialty stores and online. See Sources, page 198.

INSTANT ESPRESSO POWDER: Instant espresso powder is not interchangeable with ground espresso. Instant espresso powder easily dissolves and is great for most baking applications. The addition of instant espresso powder is sometimes used to cut sweetness, accentuate the chocolate flavor, and heighten the "coffeelike" taste of pastries. Regular ground espresso will not dissolve and can give baked goods a grainy texture. We use the Medaglia d'Oro brand in our recipes.

MALT POWDER: Malted milk powder, primarily still used to make soda fountain drinks, is one of our favorite ingredients. We use the tangy, nutty flavor of malt powder to enhance both vanilla- and chocolate-based desserts. Carnation malted milk powder is ubiquitous in grocery stores, but we also use Ovaltine chocolate malt drink mix as well.

MATCHA POWDER: At its most basic, matcha powder is essentially green tea leaves ground into a fine powder; however, choosing the type and grade of matcha is often a complex process. For the recipes in this book, we suggest you do not get too caught up in these complexities; buy the most basic of baking grades.

MELTING CHOCOLATE: You can melt chocolate quickly and easily in the microwave or in a double boiler.

In either method, make sure not to subject your chocolate to excessive heat. Also, always make sure your bowls are completely dry. If any water gets into the chocolate, the chocolate can seize up and become grainy.

Microwave Melting Method
Put chocolate chunks or chocolate chips in a microwave-safe bowl in the middle of the microwave. Microwave on high for 30 seconds. Remove the bowl and stir the chocolate (warning: the bowl may be very hot), and place the bowl back in the microwave on high for another 30 seconds. Remove and stir. Continue melting in 15-second intervals until the chocolate is completely melted, shiny, and smooth. Do not overheat.

Double Boiler Method
Fill a medium saucepan halfway with water, and place on stove over medium-low heat. Put chocolate chunks or pieces in a medium or large metal bowl, and place the bowl on top of the saucepan. The bottom of the bowl should not touch the water. Stir the chocolate occasionally (about every minute) until chocolate is completely melted, shiny, and smooth. Do not overheat.

SIFTING: Only a few recipes in this book require the sifting of dry ingredients. Sifting is the act of adding air to the dry ingredients to produce lighter cakes and baked goods. To sift ingredients, we recommend a large sieve. Sieves are less expensive and easier to clean than the special sifting gadgets on the market. Besides, sieves have many uses, and a sifter has only one.

TOASTING NUTS: It is easy to toast your own nuts. Simply preheat your oven to 350 degrees F. Spread the nuts out on a baking sheet and bake until fragrant, about 10 minutes. Make sure to cool the nuts completely before chopping them into pieces.

2

BREAKFAST

Breakfast is many things to many people. It defies, almost completely, a true definition and any set of rules, standards, and categorizations. Breakfast can be as simple as a toasted baguette with butter and jam or as extravagant as pancakes with sausage, bacon, and eggs. On the flip side, breakfast can also constitute a cup of coffee with a cigarette (the breakfast of choice of a dear college roommate of Matt's) or it might be cold pizza with hot sauce and tea (another friend's preferred breakfast of champions).

Regardless, we consider our breakfast to be morning food. Whether your morning begins at 5:30 A.M. or 1 P.M., it is the first meal you eat upon awakening. Our favorite morning meals consist of super-fresh small bites: muffins, scones, breads, and biscuits fresh from the oven. As your first meal of the day, we think it should not be squandered on tasteless bran thingamajigs, dreary wheatgrass shakes, and not-so-healthful nutrition bars (a candy bar is a candy bar, after all). A glorious baked good, like our Banana Espresso Chocolate Chip Muffin (page 32), is a wonderful thing to wake up to: a little bit sweet, a little bit savory, and almost tailor-made for a cup of coffee.

Our breakfast philosophy comes down to this: We want you to go to bed with visions of lemon loaves and marble bundts dancing in your head.

All of the recipes in this chapter are perfect distillations of our values, and they make wonderful and easy breakfast treats. Try baking a batch of our famous Easy Homemade Granola (page 47) and pair it with yogurt and fruit for a crunchy-smooth breakfast snack, or serve our Chipotle Cheddar Biscuits (page 35) with tomato soup for a large brunch gathering (the kick from the chipotle is divine). Hankering for something a little bit sweet? We think that cake for breakfast is perfectly acceptable, and our Sour Cream Coffee Cake with Chocolate Cinnamon Swirl (page 38) is reason alone to set your alarm early.

Breakfast deserves to be fun again. Share these recipes and spread the joy.

SOUR LEMON SCONES

IF YOU HAD TO CATEGORIZE OUR SOUR LEMON SCONES, THEY WOULD PROBABLY BE FILED UNDER THE HEADING "ELEGANT." They are the kind of breakfast treat you would serve for a dressy brunch or special Sunday get-together. The texture is light, and the lemon flavor is strong and tangy without being overpowering. For a special treat, serve these scones with a sweet-tart fig or berry jam.

YIELD: 12 SCONES

4 cups all-purpose flour
½ cup sugar
1 tablespoon baking powder
½ teaspoon baking soda
½ teaspoon kosher salt
½ teaspoon ginger
1 ½ cups (3 sticks) unsalted butter, cubed and cold

1 large egg
1 cup buttermilk
¼ cup grated lemon zest (from about 3 lemons)
½ cup diced candied lemon peel, optional (recipe follows)
2 tablespoons raw sugar

BAKED NOTE

The scones in this recipe are decently sized for a hearty breakfast snack; however, you can make miniature versions for a brunch bread basket. Before baking, cut the dough into 18 wedges instead of 12, and adjust the baking time slightly since the smaller scones will bake more quickly.

Preheat the oven to 350 degrees F. Line a baking sheet with parchment paper.

In a large bowl, combine the flour, sugar, baking powder, baking soda, salt, and ginger. Whisk until combined.

Add the butter. Use your fingertips to rub the butter into the flour until the butter is pea-sized.

In a separate bowl, whisk together the egg, ¾ cup of the buttermilk, and the lemon zest. Slowly pour the wet ingredients into the dry ingredients, and then gently knead the dough with your hands until the dough starts to come together. If using, add the candied lemon peel and knead to incorporate. Move the dough to a lightly floured surface. Use your hands to shape the dough into two discs (about 1½ inches in height). Do not overwork the dough.

Cut each disk into 6 wedges. Place the wedges onto the prepared baking sheet. Brush each scone with the remaining buttermilk and sprinkle with raw sugar. Bake in the center of the oven for about 25 to 30 minutes (rotating the baking sheet halfway through the baking time) or until the scones are golden brown.

Transfer the scones to a cooling rack; they can be served slightly warm or completely cooled.

Scones can be stored in an airtight container for up to 2 days.

HOW TO MAKE YOUR OWN CANDIED LEMON PEEL

4 lemons
2 cups sugar
¾ cup light corn syrup

Wash your lemons thoroughly. With a knife or a sharp peeler, peel each lemon in large strips, leaving the white pith behind; remove any remaining white pith from the peels with a paring knife.

Place the peel in a heavy-bottomed pot and cover with 1 cup of cold water. Bring to a boil and strain. Repeat this step three times.

Place peel, 4 cups of water, sugar, and light corn syrup in a medium-sized pot. Simmer for 15 to 20 minutes until the mixture forms a thick syrup and the peel becomes translucent. When the syrup has cooled, remove the peel and cut it into strips. Return the strips to the syrup.

The peel can be stored (in the syrup) in an airtight container in the refrigerator for up to 3 days. When you want to use the peel for decorative effect, remove the peel from the syrup and roll in granulated sugar. Use immediately or let dry on a rack overnight.

Substitution: Orange peel can be substituted for lemon peel in equal amounts to create a candied orange peel.

MAPLE WALNUT SCONES

THESE ARE NOT THE SMALL, DELICATE SCONES OF THE CLOTTED CREAM AND HIGH TEA VARIETY. These are hearty breakfast treats. Our Maple Walnut Scones have a toasted, homey taste and a dense texture. Serve slightly warm or let them cool and dunk them in your morning coffee as you would a donut.

YIELD: 12 SCONES

BAKED NOTE

We recommend using an all-natural maple extract in this recipe. Some artificial extracts have a very unusual flavor that can affect the taste of your scone.

FOR THE MAPLE WALNUT SCONES

4 cups all-purpose flour
½ cup sugar
1 tablespoon baking powder
½ teaspoon baking soda
½ teaspoon kosher salt
1½ teaspoons cinnamon
1½ cups (3 sticks) unsalted butter, cubed and chilled
1 large egg

1 cup buttermilk
2 teaspoons maple extract (see Baked Note)
1 cup toasted walnuts
¼ cup raw sugar

FOR THE MAPLE GLAZE

½ cup confectioners' sugar, sifted
2 tablespoons plus 2 teaspoons maple syrup

MAKE THE SCONES

Preheat the oven to 350 degrees F. Line a baking sheet with parchment paper.

In a large bowl, combine the flour, sugar, baking powder, baking soda, salt, and cinnamon. Whisk until combined.

Add the butter. Use your fingertips to rub the butter into the flour until the butter is pea-sized.

In a separate bowl, whisk together the egg, ¾ cup of the buttermilk, and the maple extract. Slowly pour the wet ingredients into the dry ingredients and then gently knead the dough with your hands until the dough starts to come together. Add the walnuts to the dough and knead gently to incorporate. Move the dough to a lightly floured surface. Use your hands to shape the dough into two discs (about 1½ inches in height). Do not overwork the dough.

Cut each disk into 6 wedges with a knife. Place the wedges onto the prepared baking sheet. Brush each scone with the remaining buttermilk and sprinkle with raw sugar. Bake in the center of the oven for about 25 to 30 minutes (rotating the baking sheet halfway through the baking time) or until the scones are golden brown.

Transfer the scones to a cooling rack to cool completely.

GLAZE THE SCONES

Line a baking sheet with parchment paper. Place the wire rack with the cooled scones over the baking sheet.

Whisk together the confectioners' sugar and maple syrup until the mixture is smooth. Slowly pour the glaze over each scone in a zigzag pattern.

Allow the glaze to set (about 10 minutes) and serve immediately.

Scones can be stored in an airtight container for up to 2 days.

FRESHLY BAKED IDEA GIMME SOME SUGAR

Flavor your morning with some specialty sugars. The following recipes will add a lot of zing to your table sugar. Perfect for stirring into coffee and tea or sprinkling on cereal and fresh fruit.

VANILLA SUGAR

Split 1 vanilla bean in half lengthwise and, using the tip of a sharp knife or a small teaspoon, scrape the seeds into 2 cups sugar. Add the vanilla bean and toss the sugar to incorporate. The vanilla bean should be completely buried. Put in an airtight container and store in the refrigerator. The vanilla flavor will become more pronounced over time.

COCOA SUGAR

In a food processor, combine ¼ cup cocoa powder and 2 cups sugar. Put in an airtight container and store at room temperature.

CINNAMON SUGAR

In a food processor, combine 1 tablespoon cinnamon and 2 cups sugar. Put in an airtight container and store at room temperature.

ORANGE ALMOND BLUEBERRY MUFFINS

THIS MUFFIN IS REALLY A NOD TO THE WAY ALL MUFFINS USED TO BE: not too large, fine textured, and full of fresh fruit flavor. The key to a good muffin is size. Muffins the size of a softball usually taste like one too. A simple burst of blueberries gives this ultra-light muffin a vaguely familiar feeling, while the orange and almond flavors provide a new spin and depth to the classic morning breakfast treat. If you use frozen blueberries, make sure to rinse them in a sieve until the water runs clear. Pat them dry and toss them in some flour before adding them to the batter. This will prevent your muffins from turning that icky greenish color and will keep the berries suspended in the muffin mix.

YIELD: 12 MUFFINS

BAKED NOTE

To finely grind almonds, put them in the bowl of a food processor and keep pulsing in very short bursts until powdered. Be careful not to over-pulse the almonds, or they will become pastelike.

Grated zest of 1 orange (about 1 tablespoon)
½ cup fresh orange juice
½ cup whole milk
2 large egg whites
4 tablespoons (½ stick) unsalted butter, melted and cooled
¼ cup sliced, blanched almonds, finely ground

2 cups all-purpose flour
¾ cup sugar
¼ cup sliced almonds, toasted
2 teaspoons baking powder
½ teaspoon baking soda
½ teaspoon salt
¾ cup blueberries
Handful of sliced almonds for decoration

Preheat the oven to 375 degrees F. Spray a 12-cup muffin pan with nonstick cooking spray.

In a medium bowl, combine the orange zest, orange juice, milk, egg whites, and butter. Whisk until combined.

In another medium bowl, combine the ground almonds, flour, sugar, toasted sliced almonds, baking powder, baking soda, and salt. Make a well in the middle of the dry ingredients. Pour the wet ingredients into the well, and stir until just combined. Fold in the blueberries.

Fill each muffin cup about three-quarters full, and arrange 3 or 4 sliced almonds on top of the batter in a floral decoration. Bake in the center of the oven for 15 minutes, or until the edges are brown and a toothpick inserted into the center of a muffin comes out clean. Move the muffin pan to a wire rack, and let cool for 15 minutes. After 15 minutes, remove the muffins from the pan and let them finish cooling on the rack.

The muffins can be stored in an airtight container for up to 2 days.

BANANA ESPRESSO CHOCOLATE CHIP MUFFINS

YOU CAN WAKE UP IN THE MORNING, PUT ON A POT OF COFFEE, AND HAVE THESE WARM AND WONDERFUL MUFFINS READY IN UNDER AN HOUR. Our recipe calls for a touch of instant espresso powder, which adds an unexpected and thoroughly delicious coffee flavor to the banana base. For those disinclined to early mornings, make these muffins the night before, as they keep really wonderfully (cool and wrap tightly in plastic wrap), and the banana flavor intensifies after a few hours.

YIELD: 12 MUFFINS

1½ cups mashed, very ripe bananas (about 4 medium bananas)
½ cup sugar
¼ cup firmly packed light brown sugar
½ cup (1 stick) unsalted butter, melted
¼ cup whole milk
1 large egg

1½ cups all-purpose flour
1 teaspoon instant espresso powder
1½ teaspoons baking soda
1 teaspoon salt
1 cup (6 ounces) semisweet chocolate chips

BAKED NOTE

Instant espresso powder is not the same as ground espresso. It dissolves instantly in hot water instead of having to be prepared in an espresso machine. It's available in most supermarkets in the coffee aisle.

Preheat the oven to 350 degrees F. Spray a 12-cup muffin pan with nonstick cooking spray.

In a medium bowl, stir together the bananas, sugars, butter, milk, and egg.

In another medium bowl, whisk together the flour, instant espresso powder, baking soda, and salt. Make a well in the middle of the dry ingredients. Pour the wet ingredients into the well and stir until just combined. Fold in the chocolate chips.

Fill each cup about three-quarters full. Bake in the center of the oven for 20 to 25 minutes, until a toothpick inserted in the center of a muffin comes out clean.

Move the muffin pan to a cooling rack, and let cool for 15 minutes. After 15 minutes, remove the muffins from the pan and let them finish cooling on the cooling rack.

Muffins can be stored in an airtight container for up to 2 days.

CHIPOTLE CHEDDAR BISCUITS

WHY CHIPOTLE? Because chipotle, when used sparingly, is the ideal way to add spice and smoke to a wide range of foods. The chipotle is just a smoked jalapeño chile, but it adds a unique personality to our cheddar biscuit. The spice starts as a small tingle in the back of your throat followed by a burst of deep, pleasant heat and flavor. Slice and serve these biscuits with a pat of butter for breakfast or enjoy with a big bowl of tomato soup for lunch or dinner.

YIELD: ABOUT 20 SMALL BISCUITS

BAKED NOTE

Chipotle powder provides a great spicy-smoky bite to these biscuits, though some people might be surprised by its intensity. Feel free to vary the amount of chipotle powder in this recipe. If you love an intense kick, add slightly more than the suggested 1 tablespoon. If you are not accustomed to strong spices, decrease the chipotle powder to 1 teaspoon.

2⅓ cups all-purpose flour
1 teaspoon freshly ground black pepper
1 tablespoon chipotle powder
1 tablespoon sugar
1 tablespoon baking powder
1 teaspoon cream of tartar
1 teaspoon salt

½ cup (1 stick) unsalted butter, chilled and cut into 1-inch pieces
2 cups grated and tightly packed sharp cheddar cheese
1¼ cups buttermilk
1 large egg
Kosher salt for topping

Preheat the oven to 400 degrees F. Line a baking sheet with parchment paper.

In a large bowl, whisk together the flour, pepper, chipotle powder, sugar, baking powder, cream of tartar, and the 1 teaspoon of salt.

Add the butter and, using your hands or the back of a wooden spoon, work the butter into the dough. The mixture should look like coarse sand. Add the cheese and stir to thoroughly incorporate it into the dough.

In a small bowl, whisk together the buttermilk and egg. Add to the flour mixture and stir until just incorporated. Do not overmix.

Use a small ice cream scoop or a ¼-cup measuring cup to scoop the dough and drop it in mounds onto the prepared baking sheet about 2 inches apart. Sprinkle with kosher salt and bake in the center of the oven for about 20 minutes, rotating the baking sheet halfway through the baking time, until golden brown and a toothpick inserted in the center of a biscuit comes out clean.

Transfer the biscuits to a cooling rack. The biscuits can be served slightly warm or at room temperature (we like them slightly warm).

Store the biscuits in an airtight container for up to 2 days.

MARBLE BUNDT CAKE

HOW DID MARBLE BUNDT CAKES BECOME SO DULL? The cake—it is cake, so don't kid yourself—should be a delight to eat. It is the ultimate coffee accompaniment, and when made correctly it is the perfect yin-yang dessert. Unfortunately, many marble cakes lack any distinction between the chocolate and vanilla components; the chocolate flavor is no more interesting than brown food coloring. Our recipe is a tribute to the classic marble bundt, with a rich chocolate flavor (thanks to the combination of dark chocolate and cocoa powder) that contrasts nicely with the delicate vanilla swirl. If you're going to eat cake for breakfast, it should be this one.

YIELD: 1 (10-INCH) BUNDT CAKE

BAKED NOTE

Many bundt pans have interesting and intricate shapes that are difficult to butter and flour thoroughly. We recommend using a nonstick vegetable spray to coat the inside of the bundt pan to ensure that the cake is easy to dislodge.

FOR THE CHOCOLATE SWIRL

6 ounces dark chocolate (60 to 72% cacao), coarsely chopped
1 teaspoon unsweetened dark cocoa powder (like Valrhona)

FOR THE SOUR CREAM CAKE

3½ cups all-purpose flour
1½ teaspoons baking powder
1½ teaspoons baking soda
½ teaspoon salt
1 cup (2 sticks) unsalted butter, soft but cool, cut into 1-inch pieces
2¼ cups sugar
4 large eggs
16 ounces sour cream
1½ teaspoons pure vanilla extract

MAKE THE CHOCOLATE SWIRL

In the top of a double boiler over simmering water, melt the chocolate. When the chocolate is completely smooth, add the cocoa powder and whisk until thoroughly incorporated. Remove the bowl from the heat and set aside.

MAKE THE SOUR CREAM CAKE

Preheat the oven to 350 degrees F. Spray the inside of a 10-inch bundt pan with nonstick cooking spray.

Sift the flour, baking powder, baking soda, and salt together into a medium bowl.

In the bowl of an electric mixer fitted with the paddle attachment, cream the butter until smooth and ribbonlike. Scrape down the bowl and add the sugar. Beat until the mixture is smooth and fluffy. Add the eggs, one at a time, beating well after each addition. Scrape down the bowl and mix for 30 seconds.

Add the sour cream and vanilla and beat just until incorporated. Add the dry ingredients in three additions, scraping down the bowl before each addition and beating only until each addition is just incorporated. Do not overmix.

Pour one third of the cake batter into the chocolate swirl mixture. Use a spatula to combine the chocolate mixture and the batter to make a smooth chocolate batter.

Spread half of the remaining plain cake batter in the prepared pan. Use an ice cream scoop to dollop the chocolate cake batter directly on top of the plain cake batter. The dollops will touch and mostly cover the plain batter, but some plain batter will peek through. Use a butter knife to swirl the chocolate and plain batter together. Pour the remaining plain batter on top of the chocolate layer and smooth it out. Once again, use the knife to pull through the layers to create a swirl.

Bake in the center of the oven for about 1 hour, rotating the pan halfway through the baking time, or until a sharp knife inserted in the center of the cake comes out clean.

Remove from the oven and let the cake cool in the pan on a wire rack for 30 minutes. Use a knife to loosen the edges of the cake and invert it onto the wire rack and let cool. Serve warm or at room temperature.

The cake will keep for 3 days, tightly covered, at room temperature.

FRESHLY BAKED IDEA BETTER BUTTERS

Make your butter better. Toasted breads, hot biscuits, and warm scones just wouldn't be the same without butter. Try one of our quick butter recipes to enhance your butter dish.

HONEY BUTTER

Place 1 stick softened unsalted butter in the bowl of a standing mixer fitted with the paddle attachment. Beat until soft and light. Add 2 tablespoons good-quality honey and beat again until combined. Scrape the butter into a small ceramic ramekin. Cover the ramekin with plastic and refrigerate until ready to use.

BERRY BUTTER

Follow the instructions above, but instead of adding honey, add ¼ cup of your favorite berries and beat until well combined.

SOUR CREAM COFFEE CAKE WITH CHOCOLATE CINNAMON SWIRL

NO, THIS IS NOT THE MOST NUTRITIOUS BREAKFAST, BUT IT IS WELL WORTH THE INDULGENCE (at the bakery we tend to indulge more often than not). Though decidedly a "breakfast" treat, there is absolutely no reason why it cannot be served throughout the day or as an afternoon snack. Obviously, part of the charm of any coffee cake is the crumb topping. Our topping is, well, tops. It is not overly sweet or ridiculously abundant; this cake has the perfect ratio of moist cake to crumbly topping, and we know you'll enjoy it as much as we do.

YIELD: 1 (9-BY-13-INCH) CAKE

FOR THE CRUMB TOPPING

¾ cup all-purpose flour

¾ cup firmly packed dark brown sugar

½ teaspoon salt

¾ cup pecans, toasted

6 tablespoons unsalted butter, cold, cut into 1-inch cubes

FOR THE CHOCOLATE CINNAMON SWIRL

½ cup sugar

1 teaspoon dark unsweetened cocoa powder

1 teaspoon cinnamon

FOR THE SOUR CREAM CAKE

3 ½ cups all-purpose flour

1 teaspoon baking powder

1 ½ teaspoons baking soda

½ teaspoon salt

1 cup (2 sticks) unsalted butter, soft but cool, cut into 1-inch pieces

2 ¼ cups sugar

4 large eggs

16 ounces sour cream

1 ½ teaspoons pure vanilla extract

BAKED NOTE

The sour cream gives this cake a tangy flavor and tender, moist crumb. Though some similar recipes suggest you substitute low-fat sour cream or yogurt to reduce calories, this is not one of those recipes.

MAKE THE CRUMB TOPPING

Put the flour, sugar, and salt in a food processor and pulse for 5 seconds to mix. Add the pecans and pulse until the pecans are finely chopped and thoroughly incorporated.

Add the butter and pulse until combined. The mixture will look like very coarse sand. Cover with plastic wrap and set aside in the refrigerator.

MAKE THE CHOCOLATE CINNAMON SWIRL

In a small bowl, whisk together the sugar, cocoa powder, and cinnamon and set aside.

MAKE THE SOUR CREAM CAKE

Preheat the oven to 350 degrees F. Butter a 9-by-13-inch baking pan. If you use a metal pan, the edges of the cake will be crispy (not altogether a bad thing).

Sift the flour, baking powder, baking soda, and salt together into a medium bowl.

In the bowl of an electric mixer fitted with the paddle attachment, cream the butter until smooth and ribbonlike. Scrape down the bowl and add the sugar. Beat until the mixture is smooth and starts to look fluffy. Add the eggs, one at a time, beating well after each addition. Scrape down the bowl and mix again for 30 seconds.

Add the sour cream and vanilla and beat just until incorporated. Add the dry ingredients in three additions, scraping down the bowl before each addition and beating only until each addition is just incorporated. Do not overmix.

Pour one third of the cake batter into the prepared pan. Use an offset spatula to spread the batter evenly.

Sprinkle half the chocolate cinnamon swirl mixture over the batter, covering the entire surface of the batter. Spoon half of the remaining batter over the swirl mixture and spread it evenly. Top with the remaining swirl mixture, then the remaining batter, and spread the batter evenly. Sprinkle the crumb topping evenly over the top of the batter.

Bake in the center of the oven, rotating the pan three times during baking, for 1 hour, or until a toothpick inserted in the center of the cake comes out clean. Let the cake cool in the pan on a wire rack for 30 minutes, then serve.

The cake will keep for 3 days, tightly covered, at room temperature.

LEMON LEMON LOAF

SOMETIMES SIMPLICITY SPEAKS VOLUMES. Our lemon loaf recipe is very straightforward. We do not add poppy seeds, pecans, or any other extraneous ingredient. We really feel that the most important aspect of a lemon loaf is the zingy lemon flavor, and we accentuate it by using a combination of freshly squeezed lemon juice, freshly grated lemon zest, and a mildly sweet lemon syrup. The sour cream gives this loaf a subtle tang and a dense, moist crumb that cannot be achieved with yogurt. If you want to increase the lemony goodness of these cakes, add the simple glaze after the syrup has set and the cakes are cool. This loaf freezes extremely well, so you can double the recipe and make a few extra loaves.

YIELD: 2 (9-BY-5-BY-3-INCH) LOAVES

BAKED NOTE

For zesting purposes, we always recommend using an organic fruit, free of chemicals or pesticides that might reside deep in the rind.

FOR THE LEMON CAKE

1½ cups cake flour

1½ cups all-purpose flour

2 teaspoons baking powder

¼ teaspoon baking soda

1 teaspoon salt

2¼ cups sugar

8 large eggs, at room temperature

¼ cup grated lemon zest (from about 4 lemons)

¼ cup fresh lemon juice

2 cups (4 sticks) unsalted butter, melted and cooled

½ cup sour cream, at room temperature

2 teaspoons pure vanilla extract

FOR THE LEMON SYRUP

⅓ cup fresh lemon juice

⅓ cup sugar

FOR THE LEMON GLAZE (OPTIONAL)

2 cups confectioners' sugar, sifted, or more if needed

4 to 6 tablespoons fresh lemon juice

MAKE THE LEMON CAKES

Preheat the oven to 350 degrees F. Spray the sides and bottom of two 9-by-5-by-3-inch loaf pans with nonstick cooking spray. Line the bottom with parchment paper and spray the paper.

Sift both flours, baking powder, baking soda, and salt together in a medium bowl.

Put the sugar, eggs, lemon zest, and lemon juice in a food processor and pulse until combined. With the motor running, drizzle the butter in through the feed tube. Add the sour cream and vanilla and pulse until combined. Transfer the mixture to a large bowl.

Sprinkle in the flour mixture, one third at a time, folding gently after each addition until just combined. Do not overmix.

Divide the batter evenly between the prepared pans. Bake in the center of the oven for 20 minutes, rotate the pans, reduce the oven temperature to

325 degrees F., and bake for another 30 to 35 minutes, or until a toothpick inserted in the center of the loaf comes out clean.

Let cool in the pans for 15 minutes.

MEANWHILE, MAKE THE LEMON SYRUP

In a small saucepan over medium heat, heat the lemon juice and sugar until the sugar is completely dissolved. Once dissolved, continue to cook for 3 more minutes. Remove from the heat and set aside.

Line a half sheet pan with parchment paper and invert the loaves onto the pan. Use a toothpick to poke holes in the tops and sides of the loaves.

Brush the tops and sides of the loaves with the lemon syrup. Let the syrup soak into the cake and brush again. Let the cakes cool completely, at least 30 minutes.

(The soaked but unglazed loaves will keep, wrapped in two layers of plastic wrap and frozen, for up to 6 weeks.)

IF YOU LIKE, MAKE THE LEMON GLAZE

In a small bowl, whisk together the confectioners' sugar and 4 tablespoons of the lemon juice. The mixture should be thick but pourable. If the mixture is too stiff, add up to another 2 tablespoons lemon juice and whisk again, adding small amounts of lemon juice and/or confectioners' sugar until you get the right consistency. Pour the lemon glaze over the top of each loaf and let it drip down the sides. Let the lemon glaze harden, about 15 minutes, before serving.

The glazed loaves will keep for up to 3 days, wrapped tightly in plastic wrap, at room temperature.

PUMPKIN CHOCOLATE CHIP LOAF

OUR PUMPKIN CHOCOLATE CHIP LOAF RECIPE CAME TO OUR BAKERY VIA MATT'S MOTHER, GAIL. She was neither a cook nor a baker nor a kitchen hobbyist (she preferred ordering in), but she enjoyed making this quickbread, as it is extremely easy and the results are impressive. The loaf is incomparably moist, and the pumpkin and chocolate chips pair well together for the perfect accompaniment to a hot cup of coffee or tea.

YIELD: 2 (9-BY-5-BY-3-INCH) LOAVES

3 ¼ cups all-purpose flour
2 teaspoons cinnamon
½ teaspoon freshly grated nutmeg
½ teaspoon ground allspice
½ teaspoon ground ginger (optional)
2 teaspoons baking soda
2 teaspoons salt
1 ¾ cups (one 15-ounce can) pumpkin puree

1 cup vegetable oil
3 cups sugar
4 large eggs
1 teaspoon pure vanilla extract
1 ½ cups (12 ounces) semisweet chocolate chips

BAKED NOTE

This recipe does not require a mixer. It is simple and quick, and the ingredients can be whisked together by hand. Also, this loaf freezes extremely well, so feel free to double the recipe and make a few extra loaves.

Preheat the oven to 350 degrees F. Butter two 9-by-5-by-3-inch loaf pans, dust them with flour, and knock out the excess flour.

In a large bowl, whisk together the flour, cinnamon, nutmeg, allspice, ginger, baking soda, and salt.

In another large bowl, whisk together the pumpkin puree and oil until combined. Add the sugar and whisk again. Whisk the eggs into the mixture, one at a time, followed by the vanilla. Add ⅔ cup room-temperature water and whisk until combined. With a rubber spatula, stir in the chocolate chips.

Fold the dry ingredients into the wet. Do not overmix.

Divide the batter between the prepared pans. Gently knock the bottom of the pans against the countertop to even out the batter. Use the spatula to smooth the tops.

Bake in the center of the oven until a toothpick inserted into the center of a loaf comes out clean, 1 hour and 15 minutes to 1 hour and 30 minutes, rotating the pans halfway through the baking time.

Transfer the pans to a wire rack and cool for 15 minutes. Invert the loaves onto wire racks and cool completely before serving.

The loaves will keep for 3 days, wrapped in plastic wrap, at room temperature.

SOUR CHERRY SLUMP

QUITE HONESTLY, WE SET ABOUT MAKING A SLUMP BECAUSE OF ITS ODD-SOUNDING NAME. Both the name and the dessert have convoluted and contradictory histories, but the slump is essentially a twice-removed cousin of the cobbler family, consisting of a cooked fruit filling topped with a biscuit crust that's cooked entirely on the stovetop. The name describes how the biscuit topping "slumps" over the filling as it cooks. We played with a basic recipe until we came up with a slump we both loved. It's very easy to put together for a quick weekend brunch.

YIELD: 8 SERVINGS

BAKED NOTE

This is a dessert that is meant to be served right away, with heaps of whipped cream or scoops of ice cream. You can prepare the biscuit dough and the berries ahead of time; when you're ready to serve, simply bring the berries to a boil, top with the biscuit dough, and 15 minutes later it's done.

FOR THE BISCUIT TOPPING

1 cup all-purpose flour
2 tablespoons sugar
1 teaspoon baking powder
¼ teaspoon baking soda
¼ teaspoon salt
2 tablespoons unsalted butter, melted and cooled
½ cup sour cream
Raw sugar for topping (optional)

FOR THE SOUR CHERRIES

2 pints sour cherries, pitted and drained
½ cup firmly packed dark brown sugar
3 tablespoons sugar
1 tablespoon fresh lemon juice
Grated zest of 1 lemon
Whipped cream or vanilla ice cream to serve

MAKE THE BISCUIT TOPPING

In a large bowl, whisk together the flour, sugar, baking powder, baking soda, and salt. With a wooden spoon, stir in the melted butter and mix until combined. Add ¼ cup of the sour cream and stir. Add a few heaping tablespoons of the remaining sour cream, stirring between each addition, until the dough feels wet. You may end up using slightly less than the ½ cup of the sour cream. Set aside while you prepare the sour cherries.

MAKE THE SOUR CHERRIES

In a well-seasoned 8-inch or 8½-inch cast-iron skillet, gently combine the cherries, sugars, 3 tablespoons water, the lemon juice, and lemon zest.

Cover the skillet with a lid or a piece of tight-fitting foil and bring the mixture to a rapid boil over medium heat.

When the mixture reaches a boil, remove the skillet from the heat and scoop heaping tablespoons of the biscuit topping over the cherries, covering as much surface area as possible. If using, sprinkle the top with raw sugar. Cover the skillet tightly and return it to low heat. Cook for about 15 minutes. Do not remove the lid. After 15 minutes, check the topping for doneness; it should be dry to the touch. (The topping will not brown the way it would in an oven.)

Serve the slump hot from the pan.

EASY HOMEMADE GRANOLA

GRANOLA, OR SPECIFICALLY STORE-BOUGHT GRANOLA, LOST ITS LEVITY SOME TIME AGO. It became a vehicle for scientifically added nutrition, loaded with additives like protein powders, bee pollens, and other questionably medicinal ingredients. Our granola is a back-to-basics whole food. Filled with nuts and dried fruits, it's reasonably healthy and wholly addictive. You can customize your own blend by exchanging fruits and nuts at will. We guarantee when the aroma of toasted oats and nuts starts to emanate from your oven, you will fall in love with granola all over again. This granola is great for snacking on its own, and for layering in fresh fruit and yogurt parfaits.

YIELD: 1 POUND

2 cups rolled oats
1 teaspoon cinnamon
1 teaspoon salt
3 tablespoons plus 1 teaspoon
  vegetable oil
¼ cup honey

¼ cup firmly packed light brown sugar
1 teaspoon pure vanilla extract
⅓ cup whole almonds
⅓ cup whole hazelnuts
⅓ cup golden raisins
⅓ cup dried cherries

BAKED NOTE

We encourage you to stir the granola twice while baking; however, if you are the type of person who really craves a clumpy granola, stir and flip a little less vigorously throughout the cooking process.

Preheat the oven to 325 degrees F. Line a baking sheet with parchment paper.

In a large bowl, toss the oats with the cinnamon and salt.

In a medium bowl, stir together the oil, honey, brown sugar, and vanilla. Whisk until completely combined.

Pour the honey mixture over the oats mixture and use your hands to combine them: Gather up some of the mixture in each hand, and make a fist. Repeat until all of the oats are coated with the honey mixture.

Pour the mixture onto the prepared baking sheet. Spread it out evenly, but leave a few clumps here and there for texture.

Bake for 10 minutes, then remove from the oven and use a metal spatula to lift and flip the granola. Sprinkle the almonds over the granola and return the baking sheet to the oven.

Bake for 5 minutes, then remove from the oven and use a metal spatula to lift and flip the granola. Sprinkle the hazelnuts over the granola and return the baking sheet to the oven.

Bake for 10 minutes, then remove from the oven. Let cool completely. Sprinkle the raisins and cherries over the granola and use your hands to transfer it to an airtight container. The granola will keep for 1 week.

Making your own homemade cake is making a statement. A smooth-surfaced, naturally colored, minimally filled cake suggests a modernist aesthetic, while a heavily decorated, loudly colored, thickly filled cake suggests a rather robust personality. Your cake is a reflection of you.

Cakes come in many shapes, sizes, textures, and varieties, but we generally prefer to bake in three styles: the towering round three-layer cake, the big hearty bundt cake, and the omnipresent cupcake. Three-layer cakes are impressive in stature, and they provide the perfect ratio of cake to icing to filling. Bundt cakes are perfect for displaying a singular flavor, such as in our Root Beer Bundt Cake (page 87), and the bundt pan provides an evenly textured and distinct crumb. And cupcakes, if made properly, can transcend the cupcake fad mania and become a surprising dessert unto themselves. Cupcakes don't have to be cute; they just have to be good.

Frostings and fillings are an important part of the cake composition. A good frosting should not overwhelm the cake layers. It should complement them. There is no reason to make a beautiful cake and destroy it with one of those greasy butter, confectioners' sugar, and (gulp) shortening mixtures. Perhaps there is some "Grandma used to make this frosting" nostalgia going on here, but we think that either a simple boiled frosting or a whipped ganache (a mixture of chocolate and cream) is the best complement to any cake. Neither requires much more effort than a confectioners' sugar–butter frosting.

Many of our cakes are curious riffs on classic candies and retro desserts, and, though whimsically inspired, our cakes are suitable for any occasion or affair. Our Milk Chocolate Malt Ball Cake (page 60) is an homage to Whoppers malted milk balls, and our Grasshopper Cake (page 57) was inspired by the nuclear-green drink and pie of the same name. The Coconut Snowball Cupcakes (page 73) are a nod to the Hostess Sno Ball, though with a grown-up sensibility. All of our cakes are artfully crafted to create a taste that is at once subtly nostalgic and completely unique.

Use only high-quality ingredients (dark, rich cocoa powders, real bourbon, pure vanilla, fresh eggs) and pay special attention to the temperature of ingredients and the texture of the batter, and you will produce a spectacular cake. A cake you can call your own—a cake that represents you.

FLOURLESS CHOCOLATE CAKE WITH CHOCOLATE GANACHE GLAZE

THE BEAUTY OF A FLOURLESS CHOCOLATE CAKE IS THAT IT WORKS WELL ON TWO COMPLETELY DIFFERENT LEVELS. First, it is very elegant, rich, and bursting with deep chocolate flavor. It can be served at the swankiest of affairs at the end of a serious meal with a great glass of red wine. This is not really a picnic dessert, if you know what we mean. Second, it is a great dessert for those allergic to wheat, as it is completely gluten-free. There are few baked desserts that taste great and are truly gluten-free, and this is one of them.

YIELD: 1 (9-INCH) CAKE

BAKED NOTE

This cake is very dense and fudgelike, and it tastes equally delicious without the glaze. Serve the cake plain or with fresh whipped cream, ice cream, or a dusting of confectioners' sugar.

FOR THE FLOURLESS CHOCOLATE CAKE

10 ounces dark chocolate (60 to 70% cacao), coarsely chopped
10 tablespoons unsalted butter, softened
1 cup sugar
7 large eggs, separated
1 teaspoon pure vanilla extract
1 teaspoon salt

FOR THE CHOCOLATE GANACHE GLAZE

9 ounces dark chocolate (60 to 72% cacao), coarsely chopped
½ cup heavy cream
¼ cup light corn syrup
1 tablespoon coffee-flavored liqueur (such as Kahlúa), optional

MAKE THE FLOURLESS CHOCOLATE CAKE

Preheat the oven to 350 F. Generously butter the sides and bottom of a 9-inch springform pan. Line the bottom of the pan with parchment paper and butter the parchment.

Using a double boiler or a microwave (see page 23), melt the chocolate and set it aside to cool.

In the bowl of an electric mixer fitted with the paddle attachment, beat the butter and sugar together on high speed until pale, light, and thoroughly combined, about 5 minutes.

With the mixer on low speed, add the egg yolks, beating well after each addition. After all the egg yolks have been incorporated, scrape down the bowl and beat for 10 more seconds. Add the cooled chocolate and mix until thoroughly combined. Scrape down the bowl, add the vanilla, and beat until just incorporated.

In a large bowl, whisk the egg whites and salt until stiff peaks form. Scoop 1 cup of the egg whites into the chocolate mixture. Use a rubber spatula to gently fold the egg whites into the chocolate mixture. After about 30 seconds of folding, add the remaining egg whites and gently fold in until almost completely combined. Do not rush the folding process.

Pour into the prepared pan and use an offset spatula to smooth the top. Bake for 30 to 35 minutes, until the top of the cake seems set or firm to the touch. Be careful not to overbake this cake.

Transfer to a wire rack and let cool completely. Use a small knife to loosen the cake from the sides of the pan. Remove the springform sides. Invert the cake onto the rack, peel off the parchment, and flip the cake back upright using the bottom of a 9-inch cake pan, your hands, or another cooling rack.

MAKE THE CHOCOLATE GANACHE GLAZE

Put the chocolate in a large heatproof bowl and set aside.

In a small saucepan over medium heat, combine the cream and corn syrup and bring just to a boil. Remove from the heat and pour the cream mixture over the chocolate. Let stand for 2 minutes, then, starting in the center of the bowl and working your way out to the edges, slowly stir the chocolate and cream mixture in a circle until the chocolate is completely melted and the mixture is smooth. Whisk for another few minutes to cool the ganache slightly.

Add the liqueur and whisk again.

GLAZE THE CAKE

Line a baking sheet with parchment paper. Place the cake on a wire rack, right side up, and place the wire rack over the baking sheet.

Slowly pour ¾ cup of the ganache over the cake. Use an offset spatula to smooth it out to the edges. It should not cover the sides at this point. Place the cake in the freezer for 5 minutes to set the ganache. Remove from the freezer and slowly pour the rest of the glaze over the cake. It should run down the sides and cover the cake completely.

Chill the glazed cake for 2 hours, or until the glaze is set, then transfer it to a cake plate. Serve at room temperature. Though this cake is wonderful the day it is made, its texture and flavor improve slightly overnight.

The cake can be stored, covered in a cake saver, at room temperature.

RED HOT VELVET CAKE WITH CINNAMON BUTTERCREAM

SO HOW DOES ONE EXPLAIN THE RED VELVET CRAZE? Is it because the cake is red? Is it just unwarranted nostalgia? Maybe, just maybe, it is because the taste is unique and, if made correctly, delicious. The buttermilk and shortening give this cake a "springy" crumb that pairs beautifully with our cinnamon frosting. Traditional Southern red velvet cakes (if there is such a thing as a traditional red velvet cake) are covered in a sweet cream cheese frosting and studded with walnuts. We have absolutely nothing against cream cheese frosting; we just felt the cake needed a modern makeover—a new dress, so to speak, for the Southern belle.

YIELD: 1 (8-INCH) CAKE

BAKED NOTE

Resist the urge to add extra food coloring to this recipe to achieve a redder cake. Subtlety is a virtue here. The purpose is not to turn the cake or the tongues of the cake eaters a radioactive color. The red in this recipe should be sly, smoky, bricklike, and restrained.

FOR THE RED HOT VELVET CAKE LAYERS

¼ cup dark unsweetened cocoa powder
2 tablespoons red gel food coloring
¼ cup boiling water
6 tablespoons unsalted butter, softened, cut into small pieces
2 tablespoons vegetable shortening, at room temperature
1⅔ cups sugar
3 large eggs
1 cup buttermilk
1 teaspoon pure vanilla extract
2½ cups cake flour
1 teaspoon fine salt
1 tablespoon cider vinegar
1 teaspoon baking soda

FOR THE CINNAMON FROSTING

1½ cups sugar
¼ cup all-purpose flour
1½ cups milk
¼ cup heavy cream
1½ cups (3 sticks) unsalted butter, soft but cool, cut into small pieces
1 teaspoon pure vanilla extract
2 teaspoons cinnamon

TO ASSEMBLE THE CAKE

Red Hots (cinnamon imperials) candies for decoration

MAKE THE RED HOT VELVET CAKE LAYERS

Preheat the oven to 325 degrees F. Butter three 8-inch round cake pans, line the bottoms with parchment paper, and butter the parchment. Dust with flour, and knock out the excess flour.

In a medium bowl, whisk together the cocoa powder, food coloring, and boiling water. Set aside to cool.

In the bowl of an electric mixer fitted with the paddle attachment, cream the butter and shortening until smooth. Scrape down the bowl and add the sugar. Beat until the mixture is light and fluffy, about 5 minutes. Add the eggs, one at a time, beating well after each addition.

Stir the buttermilk and vanilla into the cooled cocoa mixture.

Sift the flour and salt together into another medium bowl. With the mixer on low, add the flour mixture, alternating with the cocoa mixture, to the egg mixture in three separate additions, beginning and ending with the flour mixture. Beat until incorporated.

In a small bowl, combine the vinegar and baking soda and stir until the baking soda dissolves; the mixture will fizz. Add to the batter and stir until just combined.

Divide the batter among the prepared pans and smooth the tops. Bake until a toothpick inserted in the center of each cake comes out clean, about 30 minutes, rotating the pans halfway through the baking time. Transfer the cakes to a wire rack and let cool for 20 minutes. Invert the cakes onto the rack, remove the pans, and let cool completely. Remove the parchment.

MAKE THE CINNAMON FROSTING

In a medium heavy-bottomed saucepan, whisk the sugar and flour together. Add the milk and cream and cook over medium heat, whisking occasionally, until the mixture comes to a boil and has thickened, about 20 minutes.

Transfer the mixture to the bowl of an electric mixer fitted with the paddle attachment. Beat on high speed until cool. Reduce the speed to low and add the butter; beat until thoroughly incorporated. Increase the speed to medium-high and beat until the frosting is light and fluffy.

Add the vanilla and cinnamon and continue mixing until combined. If the frosting is too soft, transfer the bowl to the refrigerator to chill slightly, then beat again until it is the proper consistency. If the frosting is too firm, place the bowl over a pot of simmering water and beat with a wooden spoon until it is the proper consistency.

ASSEMBLE THE CAKE

Place one cooled cake layer on a serving platter. Trim the top to create a flat surface and evenly spread about 1¼ cups of the frosting on top. Top with the next layer, trim and frost the top, then add the third layer. Crumb coat the cake (see page 22) and put the cake in the refrigerator for 15 minutes to firm up the frosting. Frost the sides and top with the remaining frosting. Garnish the cake with the Red Hots and refrigerate again for 15 minutes.

THE WHITEOUT CAKE

VISUALLY SPEAKING, THE WHITEOUT CAKE IS A MODERN DELIGHT. The moist white cake is filled and frosted with a light white chocolate frosting and topped with a sprinkling of white nonpareils. It is monochromatic chic. Smooth the top, and you have the perfect snow-white canvas on which to inscribe and add decorations. The white cake is scented with just a hint of vanilla, and it has a surprising depth of flavor when paired with the white chocolate buttercream. We like serving the Whiteout alongside a Sweet and Salty Cake (page 67) for a little variety. So what are you? Vanilla or chocolate?

YIELD: 1 (8-INCH) CAKE

BAKED NOTE

Our basic white cake is the ultimate chameleon. Use it as a base for almost any filling or frosting (try the milk chocolate frosting on page 60). If you want to adapt this recipe to use as a cupcake base, include an additional egg yolk when adding the whole egg to give the cupcakes more structure.

FOR THE WHITE CAKE LAYERS

2½ cups cake flour
¾ cup all-purpose flour
1 tablespoon baking powder
1 teaspoon baking soda
¾ teaspoon salt
½ cup (1 stick) unsalted butter, softened
½ cup vegetable shortening
1¾ cups sugar
1 tablespoon pure vanilla extract
1 large egg
1½ cups ice cold water
3 large egg whites, at room temperature
¼ teaspoon cream of tartar

FOR THE WHITE CHOCOLATE FROSTING

6 ounces white chocolate, coarsely chopped
1½ cups sugar
⅓ cup all-purpose flour
1½ cups milk
⅓ cup heavy cream
1½ cups (3 sticks) unsalted butter, soft but cool, cut into small pieces
1 teaspoon pure vanilla extract

TO ASSEMBLE THE CAKE

White sprinkles or white nonpareils

MAKE THE WHITE CAKE LAYERS

Preheat the oven to 325 degrees F. Butter three 8-inch round cake pans, line the bottoms with parchment paper, and butter the parchment. Dust with flour, and knock out the excess flour.

Sift the flours, baking powder, baking soda, and salt together into a large bowl. Set aside.

In the bowl of an electric mixer fitted with the paddle attachment, beat the butter and shortening on medium speed until creamy, 3 to 4 minutes. Add the sugar and vanilla and beat on medium speed until fluffy, about 3 minutes. Scrape down the bowl, add the egg, and beat until just combined. Turn the mixer to low. Add the flour mixture, alternating with the ice water, in three separate additions, beginning and ending with the flour mixture. Scrape down the bowl, then mix on low speed for a few more seconds.

In a medium bowl, whisk the egg whites and cream of tartar until soft peaks form. Do not overbeat. Gently fold the egg whites into the batter.

Divide the batter among the prepared pans and smooth the tops. Bake for 40 to 45 minutes, rotating the pans halfway through the baking time, until a toothpick inserted in the center of each cake comes out clean. Transfer the cakes to a wire rack and let cool for 20 minutes. Invert the cakes onto the rack, remove the pans, and let cool completely. Remove the parchment.

MAKE THE WHITE CHOCOLATE FROSTING

Using either a double boiler or a microwave oven (see page 23), melt the white chocolate and set it aside to cool.

In a medium heavy-bottomed saucepan, whisk the sugar and flour together. Add the milk and cream and cook over medium heat, whisking occasionally, until the mixture comes to a boil and has thickened, about 20 minutes.

Transfer the mixture to the bowl of an electric mixer fitted with the paddle attachment. Beat on high speed until cool. Reduce the speed to low and add the butter; mix until thoroughly incorporated. Increase the speed to medium-high and beat until the frosting is light and fluffy.

Add the vanilla and white chocolate and continue mixing until combined. If the frosting is too soft, put the bowl in the refrigerator to chill slightly, then beat again until it is the proper consistency. If the frosting is too firm, set the bowl over a pot of simmering water and beat with a wooden spoon until it is the proper consistency.

ASSEMBLE THE CAKE

Refrigerate the frosting for a few minutes (but no more) until it can hold its shape. Place one cake layer on a serving platter. Trim the top to create a flat surface, and evenly spread about 1¼ cups of the frosting on top. Add the next layer, trim and frost it, then add the third layer. Crumb coat the cake (see page 22) and put the cake in the refrigerator for about 15 minutes to firm up the frosting. Frost the sides and top with the remaining frosting. Garnish with a few white sprinkles or white nonpareils and refrigerate for 15 minutes to firm up the finished cake.

This cake will keep beautifully in a cake saver at room temperature (cool and humidity free) for up to 3 days. If your room is not cool, place the cake in a cake saver and refrigerate for up to 3 days. Remove the cake from the refrigerator and let it sit at room temperature for at least 2 hours before serving.

GRASSHOPPER CAKE

THE GRASSHOPPER, MADE WITH CRÈME DE MENTHE, CRÈME DE CACAO, AND HEAVY CREAM, IS A NEON-GREEN COCKTAIL with no particular noteworthiness other than its color and the fact that it's the only cocktail we know of that features one of the all-time great flavor pairings, chocolate and mint. Hence our almost unreasonable fixation with the drink. At one point, probably in the 1950s, this drink evolved into a strange and boozy pie, and we decided to develop that incarnation into a delicious cake.

YIELD: 1 (8-INCH) CAKE

BAKED NOTE

If you want to make the cake kid friendly (that is, without the booze), you can substitute 1 tablespoon pure vanilla extract and 1 teaspoon green gel food coloring for the crème de menthe in the buttercream. Omit the crème de menthe in the ganache.

FOR THE CLASSIC CHOCOLATE CAKE LAYERS

¾ cup dark unsweetened cocoa powder
1¼ cups hot water
⅔ cup sour cream
2⅔ cups all-purpose flour
2 teaspoons baking powder
1 teaspoon baking soda
½ teaspoon salt
¾ cup (1½ sticks) unsalted butter, softened
½ cup vegetable shortening
1½ cups granulated sugar
1 cup firmly packed dark brown sugar
3 large eggs, at room temperature
1 tablespoon pure vanilla extract

FOR THE CRÈME DE MENTHE BUTTERCREAM

2¼ cups sugar
½ cup all-purpose flour
2¼ cups milk
½ cup heavy cream
4½ sticks unsalted butter, soft but cool, cut into small pieces
2 tablespoons crème de menthe
2¼ teaspoons peppermint extract
16 chocolate wafer cookies, homemade or store bought (such as Nabisco or Newman's Own), optional

FOR THE MINT CHOCOLATE GANACHE

6 ounces dark chocolate (60 to 72% cacao), coarsely chopped
½ cup heavy cream
1 tablespoon crème de menthe
½ teaspoon peppermint extract

MAKE THE CLASSIC CHOCOLATE CAKE LAYERS

Preheat the oven to 325 degrees F. Butter three 8-inch round cake pans, line the bottoms with parchment paper, and butter the parchment. Dust with flour, and knock out the excess flour.

In a medium bowl, combine the cocoa powder, hot water, and sour cream and set aside to cool.

Sift the flour, baking powder, baking soda, and salt together into a medium bowl and set aside.

In the bowl of an electric mixer fitted with the paddle attachments, beat the butter and shortening on medium speed until light and fluffy and ribbon-like, about 5 minutes. Add the sugars and beat until light and fluffy, about 5 minutes. Add the eggs, one at a time, beating well after each addition, then add the vanilla and beat until incorporated. Scrape down the bowl and mix again for 30 seconds.

Add the flour mixture, alternating with the cocoa mixture, in three additions, beginning and ending with the flour mixture.

Divide the batter among the prepared pans and smooth the tops. Bake for 35 to 40 minutes, rotating the pans halfway through the baking time, until a toothpick inserted in the center of each cake comes out clean. Transfer the cakes to a wire rack and let cool for 20 minutes. Invert the cakes onto the rack, remove the pans, and let cool completely. Remove the parchment.

MAKE THE CRÈME DE MENTHE BUTTERCREAM

In a medium heavy-bottomed saucepan, whisk the sugar and flour together. Add the milk and cream and cook over medium heat, whisking occasionally, until the mixture comes to a boil and has thickened, about 20 minutes.

Transfer the mixture to the bowl of an electric mixer fitted with the paddle attachment. Beat on high speed until cool. Reduce the speed to low and add the butter; mix until thoroughly incorporated. Increase the speed to medium-high and beat until the frosting is light and fluffy.

Add the crème de menthe and peppermint extract and mix until combined. If the frosting is too soft, put it in the refrigerator to chill slightly, then mix again until it is the proper consistency. If the frosting is too firm, set the bowl over a pot of simmering water, then mix again.

If you're using the cookies, use a pastry bag or a large spoon to spread 1 to 2 tablespoons of the buttercream onto the bottom of one cookie. Press the bottom of a second cookie down on top of the buttercream. Repeat to make 8 sandwich cookies. Put the cookies on a baking sheet and chill in the refrigerator while you make the ganache.

Leave the remaining buttercream at room temperature while you make the ganache.

MAKE THE MINT CHOCOLATE GANACHE

Put the chocolate in a medium heatproof bowl and set aside.

In a small saucepan over medium heat, bring the cream just to a boil. Remove from the heat and pour the cream over the chocolate. Let the cream sit for 2 minutes, then, starting in the center of the bowl and working your way out to the edges, slowly stir the chocolate and cream mixture in a circle until the chocolate is completely melted and the mixture is smooth. Add the crème de menthe and peppermint extract and stir until combined. Whisk for another few minutes to cool the ganache slightly, then let the ganache come to room temperature, about 15 minutes, whisking occasionally.

ASSEMBLE THE CAKE

Place one cake layer on a serving platter. Trim the top to create a flat surface. Use an offset spatula to spread about ¼ cup of the ganache on top of the layer. Put the cake in the refrigerator for 1 minute to let the ganache set. Spread about 1¼ cups of the buttercream on top of the ganache. Top with the next cake layer, trim and frost with ganache and buttercream, then add the third layer and trim. Crumb coat the cake (see page 22) and put the cake in the refrigerator for 15 minutes to firm up the frosting. Frost the sides and top with the remaining buttercream. Garnish the cake with the cookies, if desired, and refrigerate for about 15 minutes to firm up the finished cake.

This cake will keep beautifully in a cake saver at room temperature (cool and humidity free) for up to 3 days. If your room is not cool, place the cake in a cake saver and refrigerate for up to 3 days. Remove the cake from the refrigerator and let it sit at room temperature for at least 2 hours before serving.

MILK CHOCOLATE MALT BALL CAKE

THE IDEA BEHIND THIS CAKE WAS TO RE-CREATE THE FLAVOR OF ONE OF OUR FAVORITE CANDIES, WHOPPERS (OR MALTESERS, FOR EUROPEANS). We used varying amounts of malt powder and brewer's malt, and several different types of chocolate, before finalizing this recipe. We loved each and every combination (and ate each and every combination), but this one was the most soul satisfying. The taste is decidedly more nuanced and balanced than a candy malt ball—rich and warm and toasty. It makes a perfect occasion cake, and kids will love the malt ball decoration. You can find Carnation brand malted milk powder in most local grocery stores, or you can substitute malt Ovaltine.

YIELD: 1 (8-INCH) CAKE

BAKED NOTE

White cake, by nature, is delicate. When assembling this cake, the layers should be handled very gently. You might want to wrap the completely cooled cake layers in aluminum foil and freeze them for 1 hour before icing and frosting the cake.

FOR THE MALT CAKE LAYERS

2¼ cups cake flour
¾ cup all-purpose flour
1 tablespoon baking powder
1 teaspoon baking soda
¾ teaspoon salt
¼ teaspoon freshly grated nutmeg
1 cup malted milk powder
½ cup (1 stick) unsalted butter, softened
½ cup vegetable shortening, at room temperature
2 cups sugar
1 tablespoon pure vanilla extract
2 cups ice cold water
4 large egg whites, at room temperature

FOR THE MILK CHOCOLATE FROSTING

8 ounces bittersweet chocolate, finely chopped
8 ounces milk chocolate, finely chopped
1½ cups heavy cream
2 tablespoons light corn syrup
1½ cups (3 sticks) unsalted butter, soft but cool, cut into 1-inch pieces

TO ASSEMBLE THE CAKE

Malted milk balls for decoration

MAKE THE MALT CAKE LAYERS

Preheat the oven to 325 degrees F. Butter three 8-inch round cake pans, line the bottoms with parchment paper, and butter the parchment. Dust with flour, and knock out the excess flour.

Sift the flours, baking powder, baking soda, salt, and nutmeg together into a large bowl. Whisk in the malted milk powder. Set aside.

In the bowl of an electric mixer fitted with the paddle attachment, beat the butter and shortening on medium speed until creamy, 3 to 4 minutes. Add the sugar and vanilla and beat on medium speed until fluffy, about 3 minutes. Reduce the speed to low. Add the flour mixture, alternating with the ice water, in three additions, beginning and ending with the flour mixture. Scrape down the bowl, then mix on low speed for a few more seconds.

In a medium bowl, whisk the egg whites until soft peaks form. Do not over-beat. Gently fold the egg whites into the batter.

Divide the batter among the prepared pans and smooth the tops. Bake for 40 to 45 minutes, rotating the pans halfway through the baking time, until a toothpick inserted in the center of each cake comes out clean. Transfer the cakes to a wire rack and let cool for 20 minutes. Invert the cakes onto the rack, remove the pans, and let cool completely. Remove the parchment.

MAKE THE MILK CHOCOLATE FROSTING

Place both chocolates in the bowl of an electric mixer. In a small saucepan, bring the cream and corn syrup to a boil, then remove from the heat and immediately pour the mixture over the chocolate. Let stand for 2 to 3 minutes. Starting in the center of the bowl and working your way out to the edges, whisk the chocolate mixture until completely smooth. Set aside to cool to room temperature.

With the electric mixer fitted with the whisk attachment, on medium speed gradually add the butter pieces and mix until thoroughly incorporated. The frosting should be completely smooth and have a silky look.

ASSEMBLE THE CAKE

Refrigerate the frosting for a few minutes (but no more), until it can hold its shape. Place one cake layer on a serving platter. Trim the top to create a flat surface and evenly spread about 1¼ cups of the frosting on top. Top with the next layer, trim and frost the top, then add the third layer and trim. Crumb coat the cake (see page 22) and put the cake in the refrigerator for 15 minutes to firm up the frosting. Frost the sides and top with the remaining frosting. Garnish the cake with the malted milk balls and refrigerate again for 15 minutes.

This cake will keep beautifully in a cake saver at room temperature (cool and humidity free) for up to 3 days. If your room is not cool, place the cake in a cake saver and refrigerate for up to 3 days. Remove the cake from the refrigerator and let it sit at room temperature for at least 2 hours before serving.

LEMON DROP CAKE

OUR LEMON DROP CAKE IS LIKE SUMMER SUNSHINE ON A PLATE. The cake itself is light and fluffy, and the fresh lemon curd filling adds a delicate tartness. To finish the cake, we frost it with a lemon-scented vanilla buttercream and decorate it with its candy namesake. Make this cake for a springtime tea party or for anyone who loves a tart yet sweet dessert.

YIELD: 1 (8-INCH) CAKE

BAKED NOTE

Since the Lemon Drop Cake contains curd, it must be refrigerated after it's assembled; bring it back to room temperature before serving.

FOR THE LEMON DROP CAKE LAYERS

2½ cups cake flour
¾ cup all-purpose flour
1 tablespoon baking powder
1 teaspoon baking soda
¾ teaspoon salt
½ cup (1 stick) unsalted butter, softened
½ cup vegetable shortening, at room temperature
1¾ cup sugar
1 tablespoon pure vanilla extract
Grated zest of one lemon
1 large egg
1½ cups ice cold water
3 large egg whites, at room temperature
¼ teaspoon cream of tartar

FOR THE LEMON CURD FILLING

¾ cup fresh lemon juice (from about 6 lemons)

Grated zest of 2 lemons
2 large eggs
7 large egg yolks
¾ cup sugar
4 tablespoons (½ stick) butter, at room temperature

FOR THE LEMON DROP FROSTING

1½ cups sugar
⅓ cup all-purpose flour
1½ cups milk
⅓ cup heavy cream
1½ cups (3 sticks) unsalted butter, soft but cool, cut into small pieces
1 teaspoon pure vanilla extract
½ cup lemon curd

TO ASSEMBLE THE CAKE

8 mini lemon candies

MAKE THE LEMON CAKE LAYERS

Preheat the oven to 325 degrees F. Butter three 8-inch round cake pans, line the bottoms with parchment, and butter the parchment. Dust with flour, and knock out the excess flour.

In a large bowl, sift the flours, baking powder, baking soda, and salt together. Set aside.

In the bowl of an electric mixer fitted with the paddle attachment, beat the butter and shortening on medium speed until creamy, 3 to 4 minutes. Add the sugar, vanilla, and lemon zest and beat on medium speed until fluffy, about 3 minutes. Scrape down the sides and bottom of the bowl, add the egg, and beat just until combined. Reduce the speed to low. Add the flour mixture, alternating with the ice water, in three separate additions, begining and ending with the flour mixture. Scrape down the bowl, then mix on low speed for a few more seconds.

In a clean bowl, whisk the egg whites and cream of tartar until soft peaks form. Do not overbeat. Gently fold the egg whites into the batter.

Divide the batter among the prepared pans and smooth the tops. Bake for 40 to 45 minutes, rotating the pans halfway through the baking time, until a toothpick inserted in the center of each cake comes out clean. Transfer the cakes to a wire rack and let cool for 20 minutes. Invert the cakes onto the rack, remove the pans, and let cool completely. Remove the parchment.

MAKE THE LEMON CURD FILLING

In a small bowl, pour the lemon juice over the lemon zest and let stand for 10 minutes to soften the zest.

In a nonreactive bowl whisk the eggs, egg yolks, and sugar until combined. Add the lemon zest and lemon juice to the egg mixture and whisk until just combined.

Place your bowl containing the egg mixture over a double boiler. Continuously stir the mixture with a heatproof spatula until the mixture has thickened to a pudding-like texture, about 6 minutes.

Remove the bowl from the heat and whisk in the butter until emulsified. Strain the mixture through a fine-mesh sieve. Take a sheet of plastic wrap and press it into the mixture and around the bowl so that the curd does not form a skin.

Set the lemon curd aside while you make the frosting. Do not refrigerate the curd unless you are saving it for future use.

MAKE THE LEMON DROP FROSTING

In a medium heavy-bottomed saucepan, whisk the sugar and flour together. Add the milk and cream and cook over medium heat, whisking occasionally, until the mixture comes to a boil and has thickened, about 20 minutes.

Transfer the mixture to the bowl of an electric mixer fitted with the paddle attachment. Beat on high speed until cool. Reduce the speed to low and add the butter; mix until thoroughly incorporated. Increase the speed to medium-high and beat until the frosting is light and fluffy.

Add the vanilla extract and ½ cup of the freshly made lemon curd and continue mixing until combined. If the frosting is too soft, put it in the refrigerator to chill slightly then mix again until it is the proper consistency. If the frosting is too firm place the bowl over a pot of simmering water and beat with a wooden spoon until it is the proper consistency.

ASSEMBLE THE CAKE

Refrigerate the frosting for a few minutes (but no more) until it can hold its shape. Place one cake layer on a serving platter. Trim the top to create a flat surface and evenly spread about 1 cup of the remaining lemon curd on top. Add the next layer, trim, and fill with 1 cup of the lemon curd, then add the third layer and trim. Crumb coat the cake (see page 22) and refrigerate for about 15 minutes. Frost the sides and top of the cake with the frosting. Garnish with the candies and refrigerate for 15 minutes to firm up the finished cake.

This cake will keep beautifully in a cake saver at room temperature (cool and humidity free) for up to 3 days. If your room is not cool, place the cake in a cake saver and refrigerate for up to 3 days. Remove the cake from the refrigerator and let it sit at room temperature for at least 2 hours before serving.

SWEET AND SALTY CAKE

THIS IS OUR SIGNATURE CREATION, OUR MOST LOVED CAKE, AND OUR MOST REQUESTED RECIPE. Is all this attention warranted? Absolutely. Our Sweet and Salty Cake is an indulgent but sophisticated adult sweet: The perfectly salted caramel contrasts beautifully with the rich chocolate layers, giving the cake balance and character. It probably goes without saying that the salted caramel is also delicious poured over dark chocolate ice cream.

YIELD: 1 (8-INCH) CAKE

BAKED NOTE

Fleur de sel, or sea salt, is readily available at grocery stores; however, there is a whole world of specialty salts now available online and at specialty food markets (see Sources, page 198). Gray salt (*sel gris*), Hawaiian sea salt, Italian sea salt, and smoked sea salt will all work well in this recipe, though with slightly different (but always delicious) results.

FOR THE CLASSIC CHOCOLATE CAKE LAYERS

¾ cup dark unsweetened cocoa powder
1¼ cups hot water
⅔ cup sour cream
2⅔ cups all-purpose flour
2 teaspoons baking powder
1 teaspoon baking soda
½ teaspoon salt
¾ cup (1½ sticks) unsalted butter, softened
½ cup vegetable shortening
1½ cups granulated sugar
1 cup firmly packed dark brown sugar
3 large eggs, at room temperature
1 tablespoon pure vanilla extract

FOR THE SALTED CARAMEL

½ cup heavy cream

1 teaspoon fleur de sel
1 cup sugar
2 tablespoons light corn syrup
¼ cup sour cream

FOR THE WHIPPED CARAMEL GANACHE FROSTING

1 pound dark chocolate (60 to 70% cacao), chopped
1½ cups heavy cream
1 cup sugar
2 tablespoons light corn syrup
2 cups (4 sticks) unsalted butter, soft but cool, cut into ½-inch pieces

TO ASSEMBLE THE CAKE

2 teaspoons fleur de sel, plus more for garnish

MAKE THE CLASSIC CHOCOLATE CAKE LAYERS

Preheat the oven to 325 degrees F. Butter three 8-inch round cake pans, line the bottoms with parchment paper, and butter the parchment. Dust with flour, and knock out the excess flour.

In a medium bowl, combine the cocoa powder, hot water, and sour cream and set aside to cool.

Sift the flour, baking powder, baking soda, and salt together into a medium bowl and set aside.

In the bowl of an electric mixer fitted with the paddle attachment, beat the butter and shortening on medium speed until ribbonlike, about 5 minutes. Add the sugars and beat until light and fluffy, about 5 minutes. Add the eggs, one at a time, beating well after each addition, then add the vanilla and beat until incorporated. Scrape down the bowl and mix again for 30 seconds.

Add the flour mixture, alternating with the cocoa mixture, in three additions, beginning and ending with the flour mixture.

Divide the batter among the prepared pans and smooth the tops. Bake for 35 to 40 minutes, rotating the pans halfway through the baking time, until a toothpick inserted in the center of each cake comes out clean. Transfer the cakes to a wire rack and let cool for 20 minutes. Invert the cakes onto the rack, remove the pans, and let cool completely. Remove the parchment.

MAKE THE SALTED CARAMEL

In a small saucepan, combine the cream and fleur de sel. Bring to a simmer over very low heat until the salt is dissolved.

Meanwhile, keeping a close eye on the cream mixture so it doesn't burn, in a medium saucepan combine ¼ cup water, the sugar, and corn syrup, stirring them together carefully so you don't splash the sides of the pan. Cook over high heat until an instant-read thermometer reads 350 degrees F., 6 to 8 minutes. Remove from the heat and let cool for 1 minute.

Add the cream mixture to the sugar mixture. Whisk in the sour cream. Let the caramel cool to room temperature, then transfer to an airtight container and refrigerate until you are ready to assemble the cake.

MAKE THE WHIPPED CARAMEL GANACHE FROSTING

Put the chocolate in a large heatproof bowl and set aside.

In a small saucepan, bring the cream to a simmer over very low heat.

Meanwhile, keeping a close eye on the cream so it doesn't burn, in a medium saucepan combine ¼ cup water, the sugar, and corn syrup, stirring them together carefully so you don't splash the sides of the pan. Cook over high heat until an instant-read thermometer reads 350 degrees F., 6 to 8 minutes. Remove from the heat and let the caramel cool for 1 minute.

Add the cream to the caramel and stir to combine. Stir slowly for 2 minutes, then pour the caramel over the chocolate. Let the caramel and chocolate sit for 1 minute, then, starting in the center of the bowl, and working your way out to the edges, slowly stir the chocolate and caramel mixture in a circle until the chocolate is completely melted. Let the mixture cool, then transfer it to the bowl of an electric mixer fitted with the paddle attachment.

Mix on low speed until the bowl feels cool to the touch. Increase the speed to medium-high and gradually add the butter, beating until thoroughly incorporated. Scrape down the bowl and beat on high speed until the mixture is fluffy.

ASSEMBLE THE CAKE

Place one cake layer on a serving platter. Spread ¼ cup of the caramel over the top. Let the caramel soak into the cake, then spread ¾ cup of the ganache frosting over the caramel. Sprinkle 1 teaspoon of the fleur de sel over the frosting, then top with the second cake layer. Spread with caramel frosting and sprinkle with 1 teaspoon of the fleur de sel. Then top with the third layer. Spread with caramel. Crumb coat the cake (see page 22) and put the cake in the refrigerator for 15 minutes to firm up the frosting. Frost the sides and top with the remaining frosting. Garnish with a sprinkle of fleur de sel.

This cake will keep beautifully in a cake saver at room temperature (cool and humidity free) for up to 3 days. If your room is not cool, place the cake in a cake saver and refrigerate for up to 3 days. Remove the cake from the refrigerator and let it sit at room temperature for at least 2 hours before serving.

BANANA CUPCAKES WITH VANILLA PASTRY CREAM

PASTRY CREAM IS ABSOLUTELY UNDERUSED AND UNDULY IGNORED. This richer, sexier, silkier French cousin to good old American pudding deserves another look. In our opinion, there are few things better than a good pastry cream for slathering onto single-layer cakes or little cupcakes, or as a base for a fruit tart. Lush and fragrant, we think it makes the banana cake in this recipe shine. Its homey taste and upscale finish turn an ordinary cupcake into something special.

BAKED NOTE

Pastry cream cannot sit out at room temperature for too long; you can serve these cupcakes in either of two ways: (1) Ice room-temperature cupcakes with cold pastry cream for a nice interplay of cold and warm. (2) Ice the cupcakes and refrigerate them until ready to serve; the cupcakes become a refreshing escape from summertime heat.

FOR THE BANANA CUPCAKES

2 ¾ cups all-purpose flour
1 ¼ teaspoons baking powder
1 teaspoon baking soda
½ teaspoon salt
½ cup (1 stick) unsalted butter, softened
¼ cup vegetable shortening, at room temperature
1 ¾ cups sugar
2 teaspoons pure vanilla extract
2 large eggs
1 ½ cups mashed very ripe bananas (about 4 bananas)
½ cup buttermilk

FOR THE VANILLA PASTRY CREAM

3 cups half-and-half
6 large egg yolks
½ cup sugar
3 tablespoons cornstarch
¼ teaspoon salt
1 teaspoon pure vanilla extract

TO ASSEMBLE THE CUPCAKES

Fresh banana slices or dried banana chips

MAKE THE BANANA CUPCAKES

Preheat the oven to 325 degrees F. Line two 12-cup cupcake pans with paper liners.

Sift the flour, baking powder, baking soda, and salt together into a large bowl and set aside.

In the bowl of an electric mixer fitted with the paddle attachment, beat the butter and shortening together on medium speed until creamy, 3 to 4 minutes. Add the sugar and vanilla and beat on medium speed until fluffy, about 3 minutes. Scrape down the bowl, add the eggs, and beat until just combined. Scrape down the bowl again and add the bananas. Beat until just combined. Turn the mixer to low. Add the flour mixture, alternating with the buttermilk, in three additions, beginning and ending with the flour mixture. Scrape down the bowl, then mix on low speed for a few more seconds.

Fill the cupcake liners about three-quarters full. Bake for 20 to 25 minutes, rotating the pans halfway through the baking time, until a toothpick inserted in the center of a cupcake comes out clean. Transfer the pans to a wire rack and let cool for 20 minutes. Remove the cupcakes from the pans and place them on the rack to cool completely.

MAKE THE VANILLA PASTRY CREAM

Set a fine-mesh sieve over a medium bowl.

In a medium saucepan, bring the half-and-half to a simmer and keep warm.

In a medium bowl, whisk the egg yolks, sugar, cornstarch, and salt together until the mixture is pale, about 1 minute. Whisk half of the warm half-and-half into the egg yolk mixture, then pour that mixture into the remaining half-and-half in the saucepan and cook over medium heat, whisking constantly, until thickened, about 6 minutes. Remove from the heat and whisk in the vanilla. Strain the pastry cream through the sieve and press a piece of plastic wrap directly onto the surface of the cream to prevent a skin from forming. Put in the refrigerator for about 1 hour, or until chilled.

ASSEMBLE THE CUPCAKES

There are many ways to frost a cupcake. If you have a pastry bag, simply fit the bag with the largest tip, fill the bag with the pastry cream, and pipe out enough pastry cream to cover each cupcake. If you do not have a pastry bag, use an ice cream scoop with a release mechanism to scoop the pastry cream and dispense it onto the top of the cupcake. You can also use an offset spatula to frost the cupcakes. Top with a single slice of fresh banana or a dried banana chip.

COCONUT SNOWBALL CUPCAKES

THIS IS NOT YOUR ORDINARY CUPCAKE. It is a cupcake designed specifically for the coconut addict. Our coconut cupcakes are filled with a fresh coconut curd and topped with a flurry of shredded sweet coconut. The overall effect is a nod to the classic pink Hostess Sno Ball treat without being an exact replica (Sno Ball cakes are made with chocolate cake), and the cupcakes are a delight for adults and kids alike.

YIELD: 24 CUPCAKES

BAKED NOTE

You can easily dye the shredded coconut for the tops of these cupcakes. Just place the shredded coconut in a resealable plastic bag, add a few drops of liquid food coloring, and shake the bag until all of the coconut is evenly colored.

FOR THE COCONUT CUPCAKES

2 cups cake flour

½ cup all-purpose flour

2¼ teaspoons baking powder

¼ teaspoon baking soda

¼ teaspoon salt

6 tablespoons (¾ stick) unsalted butter, softened

½ cup shortening, at room temperature

1½ cups sugar

1 teaspoon pure vanilla extract

1 large egg

1 cup ice water

2 large egg whites

¼ teaspoon cream of tartar

½ cup shredded, sweetened coconut

FOR THE COCONUT PASTRY CREAM

2 cups half-and-half

1 cup unsweetened coconut flakes

6 large egg yolks

½ cup sugar

3 tablespoons all-purpose flour

¼ teaspoon salt

1 teaspoon pure vanilla extract

FOR THE COCONUT FROSTING

1½ cups sugar

⅓ cup all-purpose flour

1½ cups milk

⅓ cup heavy cream

1½ cups (3 sticks) unsalted butter, soft but cool, cut into small pieces

1 teaspoon pure vanilla extract

½ cup coconut pastry cream

TO ASSEMBLE THE CUPCAKES

½ cup shredded, sweetened coconut

MAKE THE COCONUT CUPCAKES

Preheat the oven to 325 degrees F. Line two 12-cup cupcake pans with paper liners.

Sift the flours, baking powder, baking soda, and salt together into a large bowl and set aside.

In the bowl of an electric mixer fitted with the paddle attachment, beat the butter and shortening together until creamy, 3 to 4 minutes. Add the sugar and vanilla and beat on medium speed until fluffy, about 3 minutes. Scrape down the sides and bottom of the bowl, add the egg, and beat until just combined. Turn the mixer to low. Add the flour mixture, alternating with the ice water, in three additions, begining and ending with the flour mixture. Scrape down the bowl, then mix on low speed for a few more seconds.

In a clean bowl, whisk the egg whites and cream of tartar until soft peaks form. Do not overbeat. Gently fold the egg whites into the batter. Fold the shredded coconut into the batter.

Fill the cupcake liners about three-quarters full. Bake for 20 to 25 minutes, rotating the pans halfway through the baking time, until a toothpick inserted in the center of a cupcake comes out clean. Transfer the pans to a wire rack and let cool for 20 minutes. Remove the cupcakes from the pans and place them on the rack to cool completely.

MAKE THE COCONUT PASTRY CREAM

Set a fine-mesh sieve over a medium bowl.

In a medium saucepan over low heat, bring the half-and-half to a simmer. Add the unsweetened coconut, cover, and simmer for 20 minutes to let the coconut steep. Strain and discard the coconut.

In another medium bowl, whisk the egg yolks with the sugar, flour, and salt until the mixture is pale, about 1 minute. Whisk half of the warm half-and-half into the egg yolk mixture, then pour that mixture into the remaining half-and-half in the saucepan and cook over medium heat, whisking constantly, until thickened, about 6 minutes. Remove the saucepan from the heat and whisk in the vanilla. Strain the pastry cream through the sieve and press a piece of plastic wrap directly onto the surface of the cream to prevent a skin from forming. Refrigerate the coconut pastry cream for about 1 hour, or until chilled.

MAKE THE COCONUT FROSTING

In a medium heavy-bottomed saucepan, whisk the sugar and flour together. Add the milk and cream and cook over medium heat, whisking occasionally, until the mixture comes to a boil and has thickened, about 20 minutes.

Transfer the mixture to the bowl of an electric mixer fitted with the paddle attachment. Beat on high speed until cool. Reduce the speed to low and add the butter; mix until thoroughly incorporated. Increase the speed to medium-high and beat until the frosting is light and fluffy.

Add the vanilla extract and ½ cup of the freshly made coconut pastry cream and continue mixing until combined. If the frosting is too soft, put it in the refrigerator to chill slightly, then mix again until it is the proper consistency.

ASSEMBLE THE CUPCAKES

Fill a pastry bag fitted with a medium tip with the remaining coconut pastry cream. Puncture the center of a cupcake with the tip and squeeze approximately 1 teaspoon of coconut pastry cream into the cupcake. Repeat for all cupcakes.

Frost the top of each cupcake with the coconut frosting and sprinkle with shredded coconut.

FRESHLY BAKED IDEA DECORATION STATION

Promote your candy from the cupboard to the counter. It's easy to create a fun, colorful, and attractive decoration station for your kitchen.

Simply purchase about 10 mini or small clear glass food-safe jars (canning jars work well), and fill them with various decorating items. Decorations might include red hots, malt balls, sprinkles of every color, Lemonhead candies, M&M's, chocolate chips, Gummi Bears, crushed Oreos, peanuts, hazelnuts, or anything else you might want to decorate your cakes with. Reserve one jar for your food-coloring gels, dyes, or pastes.

ALMOND GREEN TEA CUPCAKES (FORTUNE CUPCAKES)

THE PLEASANT GREEN COLOR OF THE BUTTERCREAM HERE ISN'T A PRODUCT OF A FEW DROPS OF FOOD COLORING, BUT RATHER A FEW SPOONFULS OF MATCHA POWDER. Matcha powder, a finely ground green tea, has a fresh grassy taste that pairs beautifully with this delicate almond cake. Top these cupcakes with fortune cookies dipped in melted white chocolate to wish everyone at your next party good luck and prosperity.

YIELD: 24 CUPCAKES

BAKED NOTE

You can order fortune cookies with customized messages or "fortunes" for your next birthday or special event. Make the message serious, heartfelt, or ridiculous. Check out the following websites: www.customfortunecookies.com and www.fortunecookiestore. com, or type "custom fortune cookie" into a search engine and browse the results.

FOR THE ALMOND CUPCAKES

½ cup sliced almonds
2 cups cake flour
½ cup all-purpose flour
2¼ teaspoons baking powder
¼ teaspoon baking soda
¼ teaspoon salt
6 tablespoons unsalted butter, softened
½ cup vegetable shortening, at room temperature
1½ cups sugar
1 teaspoon pure vanilla extract
¼ teaspoon pure almond extract
1 large egg
1 cup ice cold water
2 large egg whites, at room temperature
¼ teaspoon cream of tartar

FOR THE GREEN TEA FROSTING

1½ cups sugar
⅓ cup all-purpose flour
1 tablespoon plus 1 teaspoon unsweetened matcha powder
1½ cups milk
⅓ cup heavy cream
1½ cups (3 sticks) unsalted butter, soft but cool, cut into small pieces
1 teaspoon pure vanilla extract

TO ASSEMBLE THE CUPCAKES

4 ounces (¾ cup) white chocolate, coarsely chopped
24 white-chocolate-dipped fortune cookies (technique follows)

MAKE THE ALMOND CUPCAKES

Preheat the oven to 325 degrees F. Line two 12-cup cupcake pans with paper liners.

In the bowl of a food processor, pulse the almonds until they are a fine powder. Put the powdered almonds in a small bowl and set aside.

Sift the flours, baking powder, baking soda, and salt together into a large bowl and set aside.

In the bowl of an electric mixer fitted with the paddle attachment, beat the butter and shortening together on medium speed until creamy, 3 to 4 minutes. Add the sugar, vanilla, and almond extract and beat on medium speed until fluffy, about 3 minutes. Scrape down the bowl, add the egg, and beat

until just combined. Turn the mixer to low. Add the flour mixture, alternating with the ice water, in three additions, beginning and ending with the flour mixture. Scrape down the bowl, then mix on low speed for a few more seconds.

In a clean bowl, whisk the egg whites and cream of tartar until soft peaks form. Do not overbeat. Gently fold the egg whites into the batter. Fold in the powdered almonds.

Fill the cupcake liners about three-quarters full. Bake for 20 to 25 minutes, rotating the pans halfway through the baking time, until a toothpick inserted in the center of a cupcake comes out clean. Transfer the pans to a wire rack and let cool for 20 minutes. Remove the cupcakes from the pan and place them on the rack to cool completely.

MAKE THE GREEN TEA FROSTING

In a medium heavy-bottomed saucepan, whisk the sugar, flour, and matcha powder together. Add the milk and cream and cook over medium heat, whisking occasionally, until the mixture comes to a boil and has thickened, about 20 minutes.

Strain the mixture through a fine-mesh sieve into the bowl of an electric mixer fitted with the paddle attachment. Beat on high speed until cool. Reduce the speed to low and add the butter; mix until thoroughly incorporated. Increase the speed to medium-high and beat until the frosting is light and fluffy.

Add the vanilla and continue beating until combined. If the frosting is too soft, put it in the refrigerator to chill slightly, then mix again until it is the proper consistency. If the frosting is too firm, set the bowl over a pot of simmering water and mix again.

ASSEMBLE THE CUPCAKES

There are many ways to frost a cupcake. If you have a pastry bag, simply fit the bag with the largest tip, fill the bag with the frosting, and pipe enough frosting to cover the cupcake. If you do not have a pastry bag, use an ice cream scoop with a release mechanism to scoop the frosting and dispense it onto the top of the cupcake. You can also use an offset spatula to frost the cupcakes. Top with a fortune cookie.

 **HOW TO DIP FORTUNE COOKIES IN MELTED CHOCOLATE**

Melt the white chocolate (see page 23). Dip half of a fortune cookie in the melted white chocolate. Remove the fortune cookie from the chocolate and let the excess chocolate drip back into the bowl. Place the fortune cookie on a parchment-lined baking sheet. Once all the fortune cookies have been dipped, place the sheet in the refrigerator for 10 minutes or until the chocolate sets. Use immediately.

ICEBOX TOWERS

THE ICEBOX TOWER IS OUR VERSION OF THE CLASSIC "ICEBOX CAKE" (usually just crisp chocolate cookies layered with whipped cream), albeit a very upscale version. It is a stately dessert with a lot of visual flair, and it would not be out of place at a five-course dinner. This recipe was featured in *Food & Wine*, and we also made a mini-version for the Epcot Food and Wine Festival, for more than two thousand people. We urge you not to be frightened of lengthy, multistep recipes, but enlisting a friend is not a bad idea on a recipe as complicated as this one. For those inclined to skip a few steps, the chocolate cookies featured here taste delicious on their own.

YIELD: 6 INDIVIDUAL COOKIE TOWERS

BAKED NOTE

These towers should really be refrigerated overnight to let the cookies soften up, but if time is short they'll still be excellent after just 6 hours.

FOR THE CHOCOLATE COOKIES

¾ cup (1½ sticks) unsalted butter, softened
¾ cup confectioners' sugar
1 large egg
1 teaspoon pure vanilla extract
¾ cup dark unsweetened cocoa powder
¼ teaspoon salt
1¼ cups all-purpose flour

FOR THE CHOCOLATE PASTRY CREAM

1 cup half-and-half
3 large egg yolks

¼ cup sugar
1½ tablespoons all-purpose flour
⅛ teaspoon salt
3 ounces bittersweet chocolate, or dark chocolate (60 to 72% cacao), melted (see page 23)
1 teaspoon pure vanilla extract

FOR THE WHIPPED CREAM FILLING

1 cup heavy cream
1 teaspoon confectioners' sugar
1 teaspoon pure vanilla extract

MAKE THE CHOCOLATE COOKIES

In the bowl of an electric mixer fitted with the paddle attachment, beat the butter and confectioners' sugar at low speed until smooth. Beat in the egg and vanilla, then beat in the cocoa powder and salt. Add the flour and beat until just combined. Form the cookie dough into 2 disks, wrap in plastic, and refrigerate for about 1 hour, or until firm.

Preheat the oven to 325 degrees F.

On a lightly floured board, roll out each disk of chilled cookie dough to a 10½-inch round, ¼ inch thick. Using a 2½-inch round biscuit cutter, cut out as many rounds as you can; transfer the rounds to a large rimmed baking sheet. Gather the dough scraps, chill briefly, reroll, and cut more rounds. You should have 32 to 34 rounds. You only need 30 rounds for the towers, but a few extras are good to have on hand.

Bake in the center of the oven for 10 to 12 minutes, until the cookies are just set. Let cool on the pan for 10 minutes, then transfer to a wire rack to cool completely.

MAKE THE CHOCOLATE PASTRY CREAM

Set a fine-mesh sieve over a medium bowl.

In a medium saucepan, bring the half-and-half to a simmer and keep warm.

In a medium bowl, whisk the egg yolks, sugar, flour, and salt until the mixture is pale, about 1 minute. Whisk half of the warm half-and-half into the egg yolk mixture, then pour that mixture into the remaining half-and-half in the saucepan and cook over medium heat, whisking constantly, until thickened, about 6 minutes. Remove from the heat and whisk in the chocolate and vanilla. Strain the pastry cream through the sieve and press a piece of plastic wrap directly onto the surface of the cream to prevent a skin from forming. Put in the refrigerator for about 1 hour, or until chilled.

MAKE THE WHIPPED CREAM FILLING

In the bowl of an electric mixer fitted with the whisk attachment, whip the cream, confectioners' sugar, and vanilla until stiff peaks form.

Transfer ¾ cup of the whipped cream to a small bowl. Beat in 3 tablespoons of the chocolate pastry cream to make a light-chocolate cream.

ASSEMBLE THE ICEBOX TOWERS

Arrange 30 cookies on a work surface. Fill 3 pastry bags fitted with large plain tips with the chocolate pastry cream, the light-chocolate cream, and the whipped cream.

Pipe the chocolate pastry cream onto 12 cookies. Pipe the light-chocolate cream onto 6 cookies. Pipe the whipped cream onto the remaining 12 cookies. Stack the towers: Start with a chocolate pastry cream–topped cookie, then a light-chocolate cream–topped cookie, followed by a whipped cream–topped cookie, another chocolate pastry cream-topped cookie, and finally a whipped cream–topped cookie. Repeat with the remaining cookies. Pipe a small dollop of any remaining chocolate pastry cream onto the top of each whipped cream–topped tower. Transfer the cookie towers to a serving platter and refrigerate for at least 6 hours, preferably overnight, before serving. The towers can be refrigerated for up to 2 days.

GERMAN CHOCOLATE CAKE

THERE IS A LOT OF LORE AND MISINFORMATION THAT SURROUNDS THE HISTORY OF THE GERMAN CHOCOLATE CAKE. Suffice it to say, the cake has nothing to do with Germany and a lot to do with a waxy, sugary chocolate that goes by the brand name Baker's German Chocolate. Our version of German Chocolate Cake is really an update. We used a better-quality chocolate, increased the sugar a bit, and toyed with the amount of buttermilk until we got a moist, dense crumb. We also kept the sides and top of the cake exposed in order to showcase the wonderfully sticky coconut filling. This cake is moist and rich, and we're sure that most Germans wouldn't mind claiming it as their own.

YIELD: 1 (8-INCH) CAKE

BAKED NOTE

If you prefer to decorate your German Chocolate Cake with a milk chocolate frosting, let the pecan filling set completely and use the milk chocolate frosting recipe on page 60.

FOR THE GERMAN CHOCOLATE CAKE LAYERS

2¼ cups cake flour
¾ cup dark, unsweetened cocoa powder, like Valrhona
1½ teaspoons baking powder
½ teaspoon baking soda
¾ teaspoon salt
1 cup hot coffee
1 cup buttermilk
1¼ cups (2½ sticks) unsalted butter, softened
2¼ cups sugar
5 large eggs
1½ teaspoons pure vanilla extract
4 ounces dark chocolate, melted and cooled

FOR THE COCONUT PECAN FILLING

1⅓ cups shredded sweetened coconut
1 cup sugar
½ cup (1 stick) unsalted butter
1 cup evaporated milk
1 teaspoon pure vanilla extract
3 large egg yolks
1⅓ cup toasted pecans, chopped coarsely

MAKE THE GERMAN CHOCOLATE CAKE LAYERS

Preheat the oven to 350 degrees F. Butter three 8-inch cake pans, line the bottoms with parchment paper, and butter the parchment. Dust with flour, and knock out the excess flour.

Sift the cake flour, cocoa powder, baking powder, baking soda, and salt into a medium mixing bowl. In a small bowl, whisk together the coffee and buttermilk.

In the bowl of an electric mixer fitted with the paddle attachment, beat the butter and sugar until fluffy. Scrape down the bowl and add the eggs, one at a time, beating until each is incorporated. Add the vanilla and beat to incorporate. The mixture will look light and fluffy.

Add the flour mixture, alternating with the coffee/buttermilk mixture, in three additions, beginning and ending with the flour mixture. Remove the bowl from the mixer and fold in the melted chocolate.

Divide the batter among the prepared pans and smooth the tops. Bake for 30 to 35 minutes, rotating the pans halfway through the baking time, until a toothpick inserted in the center of each cake comes out clean. Transfer the cakes to a wire rack and let cool for 20 minutes. Invert the cakes onto the rack and remove the pans and let cool completely. Remove the parchment.

MAKE THE COCONUT PECAN FILLING

Preheat the oven to 300 degrees F. Line a baking sheet with parchment paper.

Spread half of the coconut evenly across the pan and place in the oven for 5 minutes or until the coconut begins to brown. Remove from the oven and cool on a wire rack.

In a large saucepan, stir together the sugar, butter, evaporated milk, vanilla, and egg yolks. Bring the mixture to a boil, stirring constantly. After the mixture begins to boil and thicken, remove from the heat and stir in the toasted coconut, regular coconut, and pecans.

Place the pan over an ice bath (a large bowl filled with ice) and stir the mixture until cool.

ASSEMBLE THE CAKE

Place one cake layer on a serving platter. Trim the top to create a flat surface and evenly spread one third of the filling on top. Add the next layer, trim and frost with one third of the filling, then add the third layer. Trim the top, and frost with the remaining filling.

The cake will keep in an airtight container, at room temperature, for up to 2 days.

UPSTATE CHEESECAKE

THIS DELICIOUS, DENSE, AND SUBSTANTIAL CHEESECAKE IS NOT TO BE TAKEN LIGHTLY. The recipe came to us via Schenectady, New York, from Matt's grandmother, Ann Boreali. She uses a lot of cream cheese in the filling, and the results are well worth every calorie. The thin layer of sour cream adds a nice tang, and it also conceals any cracks that may appear during the baking process.

YIELD: 1 (8-INCH) CAKE

FOR THE SIMPLE GRAHAM CRUST

2½ cups graham cracker crumbs
   (about 20 crackers)
¼ cup sugar
½ cup (1 stick) unsalted butter, softened

FOR THE CREAM CHEESE FILLING

40 ounces (five 8-ounce packages)
   cream cheese, softened

1¾ cups sugar
1 tablespoon all-purpose flour
1 tablespoon grated lemon zest (from
   about 1 lemon)
¼ teaspoon fresh lemon juice
5 large eggs
2 large egg yolks
¼ cup heavy cream
½ cup sour cream

BAKED NOTE

For this recipe, it is very important to make sure your cream cheese is softened to room temperature. Cold or even slightly cold cream cheese will require excessive beating, which could add too much air to the mixture.

MAKE THE SIMPLE GRAHAM CRUST

Lightly spray a 9-inch springform pan with nonstick cooking spray.

Put the graham cracker crumbs, sugar, and butter in a large bowl. Beat, by hand, until well combined. Press the mixture into the bottom and all the way up the sides of the prepared pan. Put in the refrigerator while you make the filling.

MAKE THE CREAM CHEESE FILLING

Preheat the oven to 500 degrees F.

In the bowl of an electric mixer fitted with the paddle attachment, combine the cream cheese, sugar, flour, lemon zest, and lemon juice. Beat on medium speed until just combined, being careful not to overbeat (too much air can cause cheesecakes to crack). Add the eggs and egg yolks, one at a time, beating well after each addition. Add the cream and beat until incorporated.

Pour the mixture into the chilled crust and bake for 10 minutes. Open the oven door to let out some heat, and lower the oven temperature to 350 degrees F. Bake until the cheesecake is set around the outside, but still slightly wobbly in the center, 45 minutes to 1 hour, rotating the pan every 15 minutes. Remove from the oven and spread the sour cream over the top of the cheesecake. Return to the oven for 5 more minutes. Turn off the heat, crack the oven door, and let the cheesecake cool completely in the oven (about 1 hour).

Chill the cheesecake in the refrigerator for 8 hours or overnight. When ready to serve, loosen the sides of the crust from the pan with an offset spatula, then remove the springform sides and serve.

ROOT BEER BUNDT CAKE

WE WANTED TO CREATE A CAKE THAT APPROXIMATED THE FLAVOR AND THE LAZY SUMMER PLEASURE OF A ROOT BEER FLOAT. We think we came close. First, we decided that the root beer flavor had to be extremely pronounced. We weren't looking for a "hint" of root beer, but an avalanche of root beer (hence the 2 cups used in this recipe). Second, we wanted the cake to be light enough for any season, so we decided to make a bundt as opposed to a larger, heavier three-layer cake. And finally, this cake had to scream for a big scoop of vanilla ice cream. Sure, this cake is amazing without the ice cream, but once the bundt is covered in its root beer fudge frosting, it would be a shame not to serve it à la mode. Make this cake the night before serving to let the root beer flavor intensify.

YIELD: 1 (10-INCH) BUNDT CAKE

BAKED NOTE

If you can find root beer schnapps, replace ½ cup of the root beer in the cake with root beer schnapps for a more pronounced flavor.

FOR THE ROOT BEER BUNDT CAKE

- 2 cups root beer (do not use diet root beer)
- 1 cup dark unsweetened cocoa powder
- ½ cup (1 stick) unsalted butter, cut into 1-inch pieces
- 1¼ cups granulated sugar
- ½ cup firmly packed dark brown sugar
- 2 cups all-purpose flour
- 1¼ teaspoons baking soda
- 1 teaspoon salt
- 2 large eggs

FOR THE ROOT BEER FUDGE FROSTING

- 2 ounces dark chocolate (60% cacao), melted and cooled slightly
- ½ cup (1 stick) unsalted butter, softened
- 1 teaspoon salt
- ¼ cup root beer
- ⅔ cup dark unsweetened cocoa powder
- 2½ cups confectioners' sugar

TO SERVE

Vanilla ice cream

MAKE THE ROOT BEER BUNDT CAKE

Preheat the oven to 325 degrees F. Generously spray the inside of a 10-inch bundt pan with nonstick cooking spray; alternatively, butter it, dust with flour, and knock out the excess flour.

In a small saucepan, heat the root beer, cocoa powder, and butter over medium heat until the butter is melted. Add the sugars and whisk until dissolved. Remove from the heat and let cool.

In a large bowl, whisk the flour, baking soda, and salt together.

In a small bowl, whisk the eggs until just beaten, then whisk them into the cooled cocoa mixture until combined. Gently fold the flour mixture into the cocoa mixture. The batter will be slightly lumpy—do not overbeat, as it could cause the cake to be tough.

Pour the batter into the prepared pan and bake for 35 to 40 minutes, rotating the pan halfway through the baking time, until a small sharp knife inserted into the cake comes out clean. Transfer the pan to a wire rack to cool completely. Gently loosen the sides of the cake from the pan and turn it out onto the rack.

MAKE THE ROOT BEER FUDGE FROSTING

Put all the ingredients in a food processor. Pulse in short bursts until the frosting is shiny and smooth.

Use a spatula to spread the fudge frosting over the crown of the bundt in a thick layer. Let the frosting set before serving, with the ice cream on the side.

FRESHLY BAKED IDEA

Do you have an unsteady hand? Is it hard for you to imagine the scale of your design on a cake before piping it?
Practice with a handy cheat sheet until you feel ready to design directly on the cake.

STEP 1 First, ice your cake so the surface is flat (or semiflat) and place it in the freezer until the frosting hardens.

STEP 2 While your cake is in the freezer, outline your cake size on a sheet of tracing paper or parchment paper, then draw your design within the cake outline.

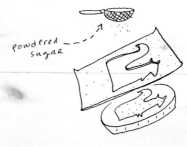

STEP 3 Next, use a very sharp X-Acto knife to cut out the outlines of your designs to make a template.

STEP 4 Place the paper gently on top of the frozen cake and sprinkle with a very light coating of sifted confectioners' sugar. Remove the paper and pipe your designs directly on top of the sugar pattern.

4

PIES & TARTS

Making your own pies from scratch is a thoroughly religious experience.

Baking a pie is easily one of our favorite things to do on a crisp fall afternoon. It is the pleasure of rolling the perfect pie dough to the perfect thickness, setting it into a heavy ceramic baking dish, and crimping the edges of the dough just so. It is the aroma of baked apples, freshly ground cinnamon, toasted pecans, and buttery crust being baked in the oven. It is the pride in serving your warm autumn pie to friends and family with a side of vanilla ice cream. Sound seductive? We offer you these words of advice before you begin.

Don't be afraid of making your own pie crust. A homemade pie crust always tastes better than a frozen store-bought pie crust. Perfecting the pie crust is simply a matter of practice and time. Our recipes for pie crusts in this chapter will provide you with enough tips and tricks to start you on your way to the pie crust hall of fame.

Give yourself some time and enjoy the experience. We've made one-bowl cakes, fifteen-minute brownies, and quick drop cookies in a time crunch, but we have never rushed a pie. It is not possible. Go to the farmers' market for your ingredients (on your way home from the regular supermarket, of course), clear out the kitchen (baking a pie is a lovely solitary activity), turn up the music, preheat your oven, and start baking.

But what about tarts?

To us, the tart is the less serious sister to the pie. Tarts are fun—more forgiving than pies—but equally tasty. The real beauty of tarts is their deceptive simplicity. A properly finished tart with a smooth ganache or prettily arranged fruit topping often looks as though it took hours to prepare, not thirty minutes. With our effortless crust recipes, it's easy to create your own tarts. Got leftover nuts, chocolate, and caramel? Perfect! Layer them together in a baked shell for a quick and easy dessert. Got some extra fresh fruit? Make a quick vanilla pastry cream (page 70) and top it with plain or lightly sugared fruit. See how easy this is?

We have gathered some of our most popular and most loved tart and pie recipes in the following pages, and we know you will enjoy them, but by all means feel free to use our recipes as a springboard for your own interpretations.

CLASSIC APPLE PIE

CLASSIC APPLE PIE IS SUCH A PART OF THE AMERICAN CONSCIOUSNESS (as in "as American as apple pie") that this iconic dessert needs no introduction. We can only offer that our recipe has been tweaked by the feedback of several of our customers, and that the magic has to do with the apples themselves. Don't bother with mealy supermarket specimens. Find great-tasting Granny Smiths at your local farmers' market, bake them in our time-tested crust, and serve the pie slightly warm.

YIELD: 1 (9-INCH) PIE

2 balls of Classic Pie Dough (page 94)
½ teaspoon cornstarch
1 cup firmly packed light brown sugar
7 medium Granny Smith apples
3 tablespoons unsalted butter

2 teaspoons pure vanilla extract
1 teaspoon whiskey
1 teaspoon cinnamon
1 large egg, beaten
1 tablespoon raw sugar

BAKED NOTE

The pastry leaf patterns or shapes you see on apple pies are very easy to make. Cut pieces out of excess dough with a leaf or other shaped cookie cutter, then apply the shapes to the top of the crust with a little water or beaten egg.

Dust a work surface with a sprinkling of flour. Unwrap one of the balls of chilled dough and put it directly on the work surface. Roll out into a 12-inch round. Transfer the dough to a pie dish and carefully work it into the pie dish, folding any overhang under and crimping the edge as you go. Wrap and freeze the crust until firm, about 2 hours, or up to 3 months.

Preheat the oven to 375 degrees F. In a small bowl, whisk together the cornstarch and the light brown sugar. Peel and core the Granny Smith apples, then cut them into ⅛-inch wedges.

Heat the butter over medium heat in a large heavy-bottomed saucepan. Swirl the saucepan occasionally until the butter begins to brown. As soon as the butter is evenly browned, add half of the apple wedges and cook over low heat for 10 minutes, or until the apples are softened.

Add the remaining apples and the cornstarch/sugar mixture. Mix until the sugar has melted, then add the vanilla, whiskey, and cinnamon to the saucepan and cook for 5 minutes, or until the filling is bubbly and thick. Do not overcook.

Dust a work surface with a sprinkling of flour. Unwrap the remaining ball of chilled dough and roll out into a 12-inch round.

Pour the pie filling into the frozen pie crust, and top with the second dough round. Trim the dough, leaving a ½-inch overhang. Crimp the edges together, brush with the beaten egg, and sprinkle with the raw sugar. Cut 3 steam vents into the top crust.

Bake the pie until the filling bubbles and the crust is golden brown, about 1 hour. Cool the pie on a rack for 1 hour. Serve warm or at room temperature.

The pie can be stored in the refrigerator, tightly covered, for up to 2 days.

CLASSIC PIE DOUGH

3 cups all-purpose flour
1 tablespoon sugar
1 teaspoon fine salt
1 cup (2 sticks) cold unsalted butter
¾ cup ice cold water

In a medium bowl, whisk the flour, sugar, and salt together.

Cut the cold butter into cubes and toss the cubes in the flour mixture to coat. Put the mixture in the bowl of a food processor and pulse in short bursts until the pieces of butter are the size of hazelnuts.

While pulsing in quick, 4-second bursts, drizzle the ice water into the food processor through the feed tube.

As soon as the dough comes together in a ball, remove it from the food processor and divide it into two equal balls. Flatten to a disk and wrap each disk first in parchment paper and then in plastic wrap. Refrigerate the disks until firm, about 1 hour. (The dough can be refrigerated for up to 3 days or frozen for up to 3 months. Thaw in the refrigerator before proceeding with the recipe.)

FRESHLY BAKED IDEA WEIGHT!

Pie weights are an essential item for any home baker. You can purchase aluminum or ceramic pie weights at almost any kitchenware store or you can easily create your own reusable (and less expensive) pie weights from your kitchen cabinet. Simply use dried beans to weight your pie crust and reuse them again and again. You can store your dried beans in a medium-sized Mason jar. Be sure to label the container "Pie Weights" for future reference.

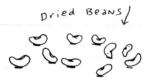

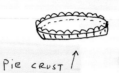

STEP 1 Buy a 1-lb bag of dried beans (kidney or cannellini beans will do just fine).

STEP 2 Line an unbaked pie crust with parchment paper or aluminum foil.

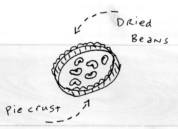

STEP 3 Pour the dried beans into the pie crust and bake the crust as directed.

STEP 4 After the crust has finished baking, make sure to let the beans cool off before storing them in a Mason jar.

BOURBON CHOCOLATE PECAN PIE

THIS IS A HEARTY PIE CRAMMED WITH THE SWEET-TOASTY FLAVOR OF PECANS AND A HIDDEN LAYER OF MELTED CHOCOLATE. Matt's dad, Larry, has a small pecan farm in South Carolina, and he is always kind enough to share his extra pecans with Baked. He was also kind enough to share his favorite recipe for pecan pie, and we use it at the bakery to this day. Larry's most important bit of advice: Be generous with the bourbon.

YIELD: 1 (9-INCH) PIE

BAKED NOTE

In our opinion, a pecan pie should be eaten within 48 hours of baking it (and there should be no reason for leftovers). Though there are people who would argue otherwise, we think that once the pie crust becomes soggy it is time to part ways with the pie.

1 ball of Classic Pie Dough (½ recipe; page 94), chilled
2 cups pecan halves, toasted
3 large eggs
¾ cup light corn syrup
3 tablespoons sugar
4 tablespoons firmly packed dark brown sugar
3 tablespoons unsalted butter, melted
Pinch of salt
1 teaspoon pure vanilla extract
3 tablespoons bourbon
1 cup (6 ounces) semisweet chocolate chips

Dust a work surface with a sprinkling of flour. Unwrap the ball of chilled dough and put it directly on the work surface. Roll out into a 12-inch round. Transfer the dough to a pie dish and carefully work it into the pie dish, folding any overhang under and crimping the edge as you go. Wrap and freeze the crust until firm, about 2 hours, or up to 3 months.

Preheat the oven to 325 degrees F. Coarsely chop ¾ cup of the pecans. Set aside.

In a large bowl, whisk the eggs until combined. Add the corn syrup, sugars, butter, salt, vanilla, and bourbon. Whisk again until combined. Stir in the chopped pecans and set the filling aside.

Spread the chocolate chips evenly along the bottom of the frozen pie shell. Slowly pour the filling on top of the chocolate chips. Arrange the remaining 1¼ cups pecan halves on top of the filling.

Bake in the center of the oven for 30 minutes, then cover the edges of the crust loosely with aluminum foil and bake for another 30 minutes. Test the pie by sticking a knife in the center of the filling. If the knife comes out clean, the pie is done. If the knife comes out with clumps of filling sticking to it, bake for another 5 minutes and test again.

Cool the pie on a wire rack and serve warm or at room temperature. The pie can be stored in the refrigerator, tightly covered, for up to 2 days.

TUSCALOOSA TOLLHOUSE PIE

TOLLHOUSE PIE APPEARS TO BE A UNIQUELY SOUTHERN DESSERT. While ubiquitous in the South (Matt discovered this dessert while attending the University of Alabama in Tuscaloosa), the pie is nearly impossible to find in other regions of the country. The pie, which is almost always served warm and à la mode, is a cross between a pecan pie and a chocolate chip cookie—a very good, gooey chocolate chip cookie. Matt's Tuscaloosa neighbor had a penchant for making a very boozy version of the Tollhouse pie, and we re-created our version (albeit with a lot less whiskey) in his honor.

YIELD: 1 (9-INCH) PIE

BAKED NOTE

We would not usually advocate the use of a microwave oven to reheat food, but you have to trust us on this: Take a day-old slice of cool pie, place it on a microwave-safe plate, heat it in the microwave on high for 15 seconds, or until the sides of the pie are warm, and serve with a scoop of ice cream.

1 ball of Classic Pie Dough (½ recipe; page 94), chilled
½ cup all-purpose flour
½ cup granulated sugar
½ cup firmly packed dark brown sugar
2 large eggs

¾ cup (1½ sticks) unsalted butter, softened, cut into cubes
1 tablespoon whiskey
¾ cup walnuts, toasted and chopped
1¼ cups (about 8 ounces) semisweet chocolate chips

Dust a work surface with a sprinkling of flour. Unwrap the ball of chilled dough and put it directly on the work surface. Roll out into a 12-inch round. Transfer the dough to a pie dish and carefully work it into the pie dish, folding any overhang under and crimping the edge as you go. Wrap and freeze the crust until firm, about 2 hours, or up to 3 months.

Preheat the oven to 350 degrees F.

In a medium bowl, whisk the flour and sugars together until combined. Set aside.

In the bowl of an electric mixer fitted with the whisk attachment, beat the eggs on high speed until foamy, about 3 minutes. Remove the whisk attachment and add the paddle attachment. With the mixer on low, gradually add the flour mixture. Turn the mixer to high and beat for 2 minutes. Scrape down the bowl and add the butter. Beat on high speed until the mixture is combined. Scrape down the bowl, add the whiskey, and beat the mixture on high speed for 1 minute.

Fold the walnuts and ¾ cup of the chocolate chips into the filling.

Pour the filling into the frozen pie shell and spread it out evenly. Top the filling with the remaining ½ cup chocolate chips.

Bake in the center of the oven for 25 minutes, then cover the edges of the crust loosely with aluminum foil and bake for another 25 minutes (this will prevent the crust from browning too quickly). Test the pie by sticking a knife in the center of the filling. If the knife comes out clean, the pie is done. If the knife comes out with clumps of filling sticking to it, bake for another 5 minutes and test again. Transfer to a wire rack and let cool before slicing.

The pie can be stored in the refrigerator, tightly covered, for up to 2 days.

FRESHLY BAKED IDEA PIMP MY PIE

Deliver your pie in high style. Bake the perfect pie in a unique pie plate and offer both the pie and the plate as a gift to your host, hostess, friend, or family member. Vintage or unique pie plates are easy to find. Check eBay listings for pie tins or pie plates, and also check your local antique markets and shops. Vintage pie plates come in a variety of styles and sizes (the pies photographed in this book are baked in vintage pie plates) and materials (glass, ceramic, tin). A distinctive pie plate is a wonderful gift for the baking enthusiast in your life.

PEANUT BUTTER PIE WITH COOKIE CRUST
AND EASY HOT FUDGE SAUCE

THANKFULLY, WE BOTH SHARE A MINOR OBSESSION WITH PEANUT BUTTER. Peanut butter on a bagel for breakfast, peanut butter smoothies for lunch, and peanut butter anything for dessert. This pie is a no-bake masterpiece and the center of our peanut butter dessert universe. The pie filling is almost mousselike and cuts easily straight from the freezer. The accompanying hot fudge sauce is the ideal over-the-top decadence, and while the pie is wonderful on its own, it is pure bliss when drenched in the sauce.

YIELD: 1 (9-INCH) PIE

BAKED NOTE

Chocolate wafer cookies are easy to find in grocery stores. Nabisco makes a fine and ubiquitous version; however, Newman's Own makes an organic and slightly less sweet cookie that we love.

FOR THE CHOCOLATE COOKIE CRUST

30 chocolate wafer cookies (about 6 ounces)
1 tablespoon sugar
6 tablespoons unsalted butter, melted

FOR THE PEANUT BUTTER FILLING WITH CHOCOLATE BOTTOM

½ cup (3 ounces) semisweet chocolate chips
½ teaspoon light corn syrup
8 ounces cream cheese, at room temperature

1 cup creamy peanut butter
2 tablespoons pure vanilla extract
¾ cup firmly packed dark brown sugar
1½ cups heavy cream

FOR THE EASY HOT FUDGE SAUCE

6 ounces milk chocolate, finely chopped
6 ounces dark chocolate (64% cacao), finely chopped
1 cup heavy cream
¼ cup light corn syrup

MAKE THE CHOCOLATE COOKIE CRUST

In a food processor, grind the cookies to a very fine powder. You should have about 1½ cups. Put the crumbs in a bowl and stir in the sugar.

Pour the butter over the crumb mixture and mix until well combined. The mixture will feel wet. Turn the crumb mixture out into a 9-inch pie plate and press it into the bottom and up the sides. You can use the back of a large spoon to even out the crust.

Put the crust in the refrigerator while you make the filling.

MAKE THE PEANUT BUTTER FILLING WITH CHOCOLATE BOTTOM

Melt the chocolate chips in a microwave oven or in a double boiler (see page 23). Add the corn syrup and stir to combine. Use a spatula to spread the chocolate in a thin layer on the bottom of the chilled pie crust. Put the crust back in the refrigerator while you make the peanut butter filling.

Put the cream cheese, peanut butter, vanilla, and brown sugar in the bowl of an electric mixer fitted with the paddle attachment. Beat on medium speed until well combined and completely smooth. Set aside.

In a clean bowl, use the mixer fitted with the whisk attachment to whip the cream until soft peaks form. Remove the bowl from the mixer and, with a rubber spatula, gently fold the whipped cream into the peanut butter mixture until the mixture is uniform in color.

Pour the mixture into the prepared crust and freeze for at least 4 hours. Once the pie is frozen, you can cover it with aluminum foil and freeze for up to 3 days.

MAKE THE EASY HOT FUDGE SAUCE

Place both chocolates in a medium heatproof bowl and set aside.

In a small saucepan, bring the cream to a simmer over medium heat. Add the corn syrup and stir to combine. Remove from the heat and pour over the chocolates. Let the mixture sit for 2 minutes. Starting in the center of the bowl and working your way out to the edges, whisk the chocolate mixture in a circle until completely smooth. The hot fudge sauce, cooled to room temperature and covered tightly, will keep for 3 days in the refrigerator. Rewarm the sauce in a microwave oven on medium heat for 30 seconds, stir, and repeat until the sauce is warm; or reheat it in a small saucepan over low heat.

Place a frozen piece of pie on a large serving plate and spoon 3 heaping tablespoons of the warm sauce directly over the top of the pie. Eat and enjoy immediately.

CLASSIC DINER-STYLE CHOCOLATE PIE

WE ARE RESCUING THE CHOCOLATE PIE FROM OBSCURITY, AND MAYBE EVEN EXTINCTION. What was once a whimsical chocolate-lover's dream has suffered from poor ingredients (enough already with all these boxed pudding mixes) and even poorer interpretations. Our version of the chocolate pie is an homage to the much-loved dessert of our youth, the one that was drenched in canned whipped cream and a flurry of chocolate curls. We updated the pie with a renewed focus on the chocolate (it's deeper and richer), poured it into a cookie crust, and topped it off with a shot of whiskey.

YIELD: 1 (9-INCH) PIE

BAKED NOTE

For a richer, darker chocolate pie, simply replace the chocolate malt with unsweetened dark cocoa powder.

FOR THE CHOCOLATE COOKIE CRUST

30 chocolate wafer cookies (about 6 ounces)
1 tablespoon sugar
6 tablespoons unsalted butter, melted

FOR THE CHOCOLATE FILLING

½ cup sugar
3 tablespoons chocolate malt Ovaltine
1 teaspoon salt
¼ cup cornstarch
5 large egg yolks

2 cups whole milk
½ cup heavy cream
5 ounces dark chocolate (60 to 72% cacao), coarsely chopped
2 ounces milk chocolate, coarsely chopped
2 teaspoons whiskey
1 teaspoon pure vanilla extract

TO SERVE

Whipped cream or vanilla bean whipped cream (recipe follows)

MAKE THE CHOCOLATE COOKIE CRUST

In a food processor, grind the cookies to a very fine powder. You should have about 1½ cups. Put the crumbs in a bowl and stir in the sugar.

Pour the butter over the crumb mixture and mix until well combined. The mixture will feel wet. Turn the crumb mixture out into a 9-inch pie plate and press it into the bottom and up the sides. You can use the back of a large spoon to even out the crust.

Freeze the crust while you make the filling.

MAKE THE CHOCOLATE FILLING

In a medium saucepan, whisk together the sugar, Ovaltine, salt, and cornstarch. Add the egg yolks and whisk until combined. The mixture will look like a thick paste. Slowly pour in the milk and cream, whisking constantly.

Bring to a boil over medium heat, whisking constantly to prevent the mixture from burning on the bottom of the pan. Boil for 30 seconds, then remove from the heat.

Add the chocolates, whiskey, and vanilla and whisk until combined. Continue to whisk for a few minutes to cool the mixture slightly. Let the mixture stand for 15 minutes at room temperature. A thin skin may form during this cooling period. Simply whisk the mixture again until the skin is gone. Pour the filling into the frozen pie shell.

Refrigerate the pie for 4 hours before serving, topped with whipped cream, if desired.

SIMPLE VANILLA BEAN WHIPPED CREAM

YIELD: ABOUT 3½ CUPS WHIPPED CREAM

2 cups heavy cream
1 vanilla bean
¼ cup sugar

Pour the cream into a medium bowl or a large glass measuring cup.

Cut the vanilla bean in half lengthwise and, using the tip of the knife or a small teaspoon, scrape the seeds into the cream. Add the vanilla bean to the cream. Use a whisk to disperse the vanilla bean seeds. Cover the mixture and refrigerate for about 1 hour to allow the vanilla flavor to infuse the cream.

Remove the cream from the refrigerator and pour through a fine-mesh sieve into the chilled bowl of an electric mixer fitted with the chilled whisk attachment. Beat on medium speed for 1 minute. Continuing to mix, sprinkle the sugar over the cream, then turn the mixer to medium-high and beat until soft peaks form.

Serve immediately, or cover and refrigerate for up to 2 hours.

BUTTERSCOTCH PUDDING TARTS

THESE ARE IMPRESSIVE TARTS THAT ARE SURPRISINGLY EASY TO MAKE. Blair Van Sant, a self-styled pudding enthusiast, devised this recipe for us. It is toothsome and vaguely nostalgic. The butterscotch flavor is simple and straightforward, and it pairs magnificently well with the oat wheat crust. The crust is fairly forgiving, and the filling is a simple (albeit addictively delicious) homemade pudding. When topped with a few crumbled pieces of a Butterfinger candy bar, the tart becomes a whimsical dinner party dessert.

YIELD: 8 (4-INCH) TARTS

BAKED NOTE

For an even simpler dessert, forgo the crust and make just the pudding filling. Serve it over vanilla wafers in individual ramekins.

FOR THE OAT WHEAT PIE CRUST

1 cup rolled oats
½ cup whole wheat flour
1 cup all-purpose flour
¼ cup firmly packed dark brown sugar
½ teaspoon salt
¾ cup (1½ sticks) cold unsalted butter, cut into cubes
¼ cup milk

FOR THE BUTTERSCOTCH PUDDING

6 large egg yolks
¾ cup granulated sugar
¼ cup heavy cream
½ cup firmly packed dark brown sugar
⅓ cup cornstarch, sifted
1 teaspoon salt
3 cups whole milk
1 vanilla bean
1 tablespoon unsalted butter
2 tablespoons whiskey

TO ASSEMBLE THE TARTS

1 Butterfinger candy bar, broken into small pieces

MAKE THE OAT WHEAT PIE CRUST

Put the rolled oats in a food processor and process for about 30 seconds, until ground but not powdered. Add the flours, brown sugar, and salt and pulse until combined.

Add the butter and pulse until the butter pieces are small and the dough looks crumbly, like coarse sand. Add the milk and pulse for a few seconds.

Scoop the dough out of the food processor and form it into a large disk. Wrap tightly in plastic and refrigerate for at least 1 hour and up to 3 hours.

Dust a work surface with a sprinkling of flour. Unwrap the disk of chilled dough and put it directly on the work surface. Cut the dough into eight equal pieces, about 2 ounces each, and gently shape each piece into a smooth disk. The dough will be sticky. Make sure to turn the dough over (use a spatula or a bench knife) as needed and keep the working surface floured. Put the dough disks in the refrigerator for 10 minutes.

Using a rolling pin, roll each dough ball into a 6-inch round just over ⅛ inch thick. Place a round over a 4-inch tart pan and very gently press the dough into the pan. Roll the rolling pin over the pan to trim off excess. Repeat with the remaining dough rounds. Use any excess dough trimmings to make a ninth tart shell or freeze them for another time.

Preheat the oven to 325 degrees F.

Put the tart pans in the freezer for 30 minutes.

Remove the tarts from the freezer, then arrange on a baking sheet and gently prick the dough with a fork.

Bake on the baking sheet until golden brown, 12 to 15 minutes, rotating the baking sheet halfway through the baking time.

Transfer the tart pans to wire racks and let cool completely.

MAKE THE BUTTERSCOTCH PUDDING

Put the egg yolks in a large heatproof bowl and set aside.

In a small saucepan, combine the granulated sugar and ¼ cup water and stir gently with a heatproof spatula; do not splash the sides of the pan. Cook over medium heat until the sugar is dissolved, then increase the heat to medium-high and cook until the mixture begins to turn a dark amber color. Swirl the pan, if necessary, to create an even color, but do not stir. Remove from the heat, let stand for 1 minute, then use the heatproof spatula to stir in the cream. Pour the caramel into a small bowl. Set aside.

In another small saucepan, combine the brown sugar, cornstarch, and salt. Stir in the milk and whisk to combine.

Cut the vanilla bean in half lengthwise, and, using the tip of the knife or a small teaspoon, scrape the seeds into the saucepan with the milk. Add the vanilla bean to the milk as well. Cook over medium-high heat, whisking occasionally, until the mixture comes to a boil. Remove from heat and add the caramel. Whisk together until combined, then pour one third of the mixture over the eggs. Keep whisking the egg mixture and add another third of the hot milk mixture. Transfer the egg mixture back to the saucepan with the milk mixture and, whisking constantly, bring to a boil over medium-high heat. Boil for 2 to 3 minutes, or until very thick.

Remove from the heat and add the butter and whiskey.

Keep whisking vigorously for about 1 minute to cool the pudding slightly. Let the pudding sit for about 15 minutes, then remove the vanilla bean.

ASSEMBLE THE TARTS

Whisk the pudding one more time until smooth. Divide the pudding equally among the tart shells and sprinkle some of the crumbled candy bar over the pudding. Cover the tarts with plastic wrap and put them in the refrigerator for about 2 hours before serving.

The tarts can be stored, tightly covered, in the refrigerator for up to 2 days.

LEMON-ALMOND MERINGUE TARTS

MATT MADE THESE TARTS ON THE MARTHA STEWART SHOW, AND THEY HAVE BEEN A BEST SELLER EVER SINCE. The light almond-flavored crust, tangy lemon curd, and marshmallowy meringue marry perfectly, and the tarts can be served for almost any occasion. Do not be afraid of the many steps involved, as they are quite easy to follow, and you can break up the recipe into two days: Make the tart dough and the lemon curd on day one, and bake the tarts and make the meringue on day two.

YIELD: 8 (4-INCH) TARTS

BAKED NOTE

This dough makes a wonderful crust for the lemon curd filling, but, like all nut tart doughs, it is very fragile once baked. Use a light hand when serving.

FOR THE ALMOND AMARETTO TART SHELLS

1 cup all-purpose flour

⅓ cup finely ground blanched sliced almonds

2 tablespoons finely ground amaretti cookies

14 tablespoons unsalted butter, soft but cool, cut into 1-inch pieces

⅓ cup plus 1 tablespoon confectioners' sugar

1 large egg yolk

1 tablespoon heavy cream

1 tablespoon amaretto liqueur

FOR THE LEMON CURD

¾ cup fresh lemon juice (from about 6 lemons)

Grated zest of 2 lemons

2 large eggs

7 large egg yolks (reserve the whites for the topping)

¾ cup sugar

4 tablespoons (½ stick) butter, softened

FOR THE AMARETTO MERINGUE TOPPING

7 large egg whites

1¾ cups sugar

½ teaspoon cream of tartar

1 tablespoon plus 1 teaspoon amaretto liqueur

TO ASSEMBLE THE TARTS

Crushed amaretti cookies, optional

MAKE THE ALMOND AMARETTO TART SHELLS

In a small mixing bowl, stir the flour, almonds, and cookies together.

Put the butter in the bowl of an electric mixer fitted with the paddle attachment. Pour the confectioners' sugar over the butter and, using your hands, toss to make sure each piece of butter is fully coated. Beat on medium speed until just combined. Scrape down the bowl and add the egg yolk. Beat until combined. With the mixer on low to medium, very slowly pour in the flour mixture, mixing until combined. Scrape down the bowl and add the cream and liqueur and mix until combined.

Using your hands, form the dough into a ball (it will be sticky), wrap it in plastic, and refrigerate for 3 hours.

Dust a work surface with a sprinkling of flour. Unwrap the ball of chilled dough and put it directly on the work surface. Cut the dough into eight equal pieces, about 2 ounces each, and gently shape each piece into a smooth disk. The dough will be sticky. Make sure to turn the dough over (use a spatula or a bench knife) as needed and keep the work surface floured. Put the dough disks in the refrigerator for 10 minutes.

Using a rolling pin, roll each dough ball into a 6-inch round just over ⅛ inch thick. Place a round over a 4-inch tart pan and very gently press the dough into the pan. Roll the rolling pin over the pan to trim off excess dough. Repeat with the remaining dough rounds. Use any excess dough trimmings to make a ninth tart shell, or freeze them for another time. Put the tart pans in the refrigerator for 30 minutes.

Preheat the oven to 375 degrees F. Remove the tarts from the refrigerator, then arrange on a baking sheet and gently prick the dough with a fork.

Bake until golden brown, about 20 minutes, rotating the baking sheet halfway through the baking time.

Transfer the tart pans to wire racks and let cool completely.

MAKE THE LEMON CURD

In a small bowl, combine the lemon juice and zest and let sit for about 10 minutes to soften the lemon zest.

In a medium nonreactive bowl, whisk the eggs, egg yolks, and sugar together until combined. Add the lemon juice and zest and whisk until just combined.

Set the bowl over a pan of simmering water but do not let the water touch the bottom of the bowl. Cook, stirring constantly with a heatproof spatula, until the mixture has thickened to a puddinglike consistency, about 6 minutes.

Remove the bowl from the pan and whisk in the butter until emulsified. Strain the mixture through a fine-mesh sieve into a bowl. Press a piece of plastic wrap directly onto the surface of the curd to prevent a skin from forming. Set aside at room temperature while you make the meringue.

MAKE THE AMARETTO MERINGUE TOPPING

Whisk the egg whites and sugar together in a nonreactive metal bowl until combined.

Set the bowl over a saucepan of simmering water. Cook, whisking constantly, until the sugar is completely dissolved and the mixture registers 140 degrees F. on an instant-read thermometer, 6 to 8 minutes.

Remove the bowl from the pan and, with an electric mixer fitted with the whisk attachment, beat the mixture on high speed until stiff peaks form, adding the cream of tartar when the mixture begins to thicken or after 3 minutes. When the mixture almost holds stiff peaks, after about 6 minutes, add the liqueur and beat to incorporate it.

ASSEMBLE THE TARTS

Divide the warm lemon curd evenly among the tarts. Use a large ice cream scoop with a release mechanism to drop mounds of meringue on top of the lemon curd. Spread the meringue out toward the edges of the tart. Add more meringue to your liking (you will have extra, which you can use to make meringue cookies; see below).

Preheat the broiler to high. Slide the tarts under the broiler and cook until just brown.

If using, sprinkle the crushed cookies on top of the meringue and serve.

These tarts should be eaten within 24 hours. If you are making them for dinner, prepare them in the morning and leave them at room temperature until ready to serve.

HOW TO MAKE MERINGUE COOKIES

This recipe makes a lot of meringue. You can pile the meringue high on your tarts, or you can make easy meringue cookies: Preheat the oven to 200 degrees F., drop meringue by heaping tablespoons onto a parchment-lined baking sheet, and bake for 90 minutes, rotating the baking sheet halfway through the baking time. Turn off the oven, crack the door, and leave the meringues in the oven overnight. For extra-fun meringues, fold ½ cup semi-sweet chocolate chips into the meringue mixture before dropping it onto the baking sheet.

PEAR PLUM CRISP

THIS IS A VARIATION ON THE CLASSIC APPLE CRISP. While almost any fruit will taste delicious with our oat topping, we think the combination of pears and plums is ideal because of the contrasting textures, levels of sweetness, and terrific color. This recipe is great for any outdoor event, and it is super easy to make.

YIELD: 1 (8-BY-8-BY-2 INCH) CRISP
OR 4 SERVINGS

BAKED NOTE

Our crisp recipe is quite versatile. For large gatherings, you can easily double (or triple or quadruple) this recipe and bake one big casserole dish.

FOR THE FRUIT FILLING

2 medium Bosc pears, cored and cut into
  1-inch pieces
2 medium Bartlett pears, cored and cut
  into 1-inch pieces
3 large plums, pitted and cut into
  thin wedges
Grated zest and juice of ½ lemon
Grated zest and juice of ½ orange
½ teaspoon cinnamon
¼ teaspoon freshly grated nutmeg
½ cup firmly packed dark brown sugar
2 tablespoons all-purpose flour

FOR THE OAT TOPPING

6 tablespooons cold unsalted butter,
  cut into pea-sized pieces
¾ cup all-purpose flour
¾ cup rolled oats
¼ cup firmly packed dark brown sugar
½ cup granulated sugar

TO SERVE

Vanilla ice cream

MAKE THE FRUIT FILLING

Preheat the oven to 350 degrees F.

In a medium bowl, using a wooden spoon, toss together the pears, plums, and the lemon and orange zest and juice. Add the cinnamon, nutmeg, sugar, and flour and stir until just combined. Set aside.

MAKE THE OAT TOPPING

In a small bowl, using a wooden spoon, toss together the butter and flour until the butter pieces are evenly coated. Add the oats and both sugars, and using your hands or the back of a wooden spoon, rub the mixture together until it resembles coarse meal.

ASSEMBLE THE CRISP

Pour the filling into one 8-by-8-by-2-inch pan, and completely cover the top of the filling with the oat topping.

Bake in the center of the oven for 45 minutes. Remove from the oven, let cool for 20 minutes, and serve slightly warm with a scoop of ice cream.

The crisp can be stored in an airtight container in the refrigerator for up to 3 days, and can be reheated in the microwave in 15-second bursts until warm.

BROWNIES & BARS

5

The perfect brownie is a topic of much discussion. Everyone has an opinion or a specific brownie memory. Brownies are eaten, dissected, and discussed. Chewy? Fudgy? Cakey? Frosting?

Brownies are our thing. We have done our brownie research. We've performed in-depth scholarly studies, and we've tested and eaten sample after sample of brownie after brownie. The fruits of our labor have culminated in our favorite brownie recipe ever (page 117). It is a great one—it's the same recipe we used to win Oprah's affections (our brownies appeared in O magazine as one of her favorite things), and it won top honors from the folks at *America's Test Kitchen* and the *Today* show—and now we happily pass it along to you in this chapter.

We also want to pass along some of our brownie wisdom. First, brownies should never be cakey. It's pointless. Cakes are cakey. Texturally, brownies should be slightly fudgy and should contain no leavening agents (that is, baking soda or baking powder), which give brownies an unnecessary lift. Second, brownies should not have any frosting. Again, a frosted brownie is just a brownie masquerading as cake. We do have a weakness for brownies enveloped in tempered chocolate, with the chocolate acting almost like a candy shell, but this is the only acceptable brownie covering. Lastly, a brownie is all about the chocolate. Do not bother making these brownies with lowly, waxy, run-of-the-mill chocolate. Use a really dark cocoa powder and a well-respected chocolate.

Oh, and about our bars. Most of the bar recipes in this book are reinterpretations of our favorite grade-school bake sale goods. The Peanut Butter Crispy Bars (page 133) are Rice Krispy Treats all dressed up in dark chocolate and peanut butter with candied crisped rice cereal, and the S'more Nut Bars (page 118) are a cross between a S'more and a regal chocolate and nut confection. Our bars are pure fun. They aren't serious or haughty; they are simply imaginative, delicious desserts that are equally at home at the neighborhood lemonade stand and at a breezy cocktail party.

Finally, most of our bars and brownies are fairly easy to make and can easily be doubled, tripled, and quadrupled for large parties.

THE BAKED BROWNIE

THE BAKED BROWNIE IS A BEAUTIFUL THING. It has won the hearts and minds of many people, it's been featured on the pages of O magazine as a favorite thing, and it was awarded best brownie honors by the folks at *America's Test Kitchen* and the *Today* show. Our brownie owes a lot to our friend and superstar pastry chef Lesli Heffler-Flick. She created the original ultimate brownie for us. It is dense, chocolatey, and slightly fudgy, and we are forever grateful to her for letting us adapt her recipe.

YIELD: 24 BROWNIES

1¼ cups all-purpose flour
1 teaspoon salt
2 tablespoons dark unsweetened cocoa powder
11 ounces dark chocolate (60 to 72% cacao), coarsely chopped
1 cup (2 sticks) unsalted butter, cut into 1-inch pieces

1 teaspoon instant espresso powder
1½ cups granulated sugar
½ cup firmly packed light brown sugar
5 large eggs, at room temperature
2 teaspoons pure vanilla extract

BAKED NOTE

A great brownie is easy to make, but here are a few pointers: (1) Use a dark unsweetened cocoa powder like Valrhona. A pale, light-colored cocoa does not have enough depth. (2) Make sure your eggs are at room temperature, and do not overbeat them into the batter. (3) Check your brownies often as they bake. An even slightly overbaked brownie is not a Baked Brownie.

Preheat the oven to 350 degrees F. Butter the sides and bottom of a 9-by-13-inch glass or light-colored metal baking pan.

In a medium bowl, whisk the flour, salt, and cocoa powder together.

Put the chocolate, butter, and instant espresso powder in a large bowl and set it over a saucepan of simmering water, stirring occasionally, until the chocolate and butter are completely melted and smooth. Turn off the heat, but keep the bowl over the water and add the sugars. Whisk until completely combined, then remove the bowl from the pan. The mixture should be room temperature.

Add 3 eggs to the chocolate mixture and whisk until combined. Add the remaining eggs and whisk until combined. Add the vanilla and stir until combined. Do not overbeat the batter at this stage or your brownies will be cakey.

Sprinkle the flour mixture over the chocolate mixture. Using a spatula (*not a whisk*), fold the flour mixture into the chocolate until just a bit of the flour mixture is visible.

Pour the batter into the prepared pan and smooth the top. Bake in the center of the oven for 30 minutes, rotating the pan halfway through the baking time, until a toothpick inserted into the center of the brownies comes out with a few moist crumbs sticking to it. Let the brownies cool completely, then cut them into squares and serve.

Tightly covered with plastic wrap, the brownies keep at room temperature for up to 3 days.

S'MORE NUT BARS

THIS IS A HYBRID BAR COMBINING THE BEST QUALITIES OF A CLASSIC S'MORE WITH A STRAIGHT-FORWARD NUT BAR. Rich, chocolatey, and both sweet and salty, it's the perfect summer dessert for an afternoon barbeque, picnic, or pool party. The recipe is hassle-free and can be thrown together in less than half an hour, then put in the refrigerator to set up.

YIELD: 24 BARS

BAKED NOTE

Chocolate desserts will absorb any and all refrigerator odors. Make sure your bars, or any refrigerated chocolate desserts, are wrapped airtight. Obviously, you do not want these bars to taste like your leftover Chinese takeout.

2 ¼ cups graham cracker crumbs (about 17-20 crackers)

1 tablespoon firmly packed dark brown sugar

⅔ cup unsalted butter, melted

7 ½ ounces milk chocolate, coarsely chopped

7 ½ ounces dark chocolate (60 to 72% cacao), coarsely chopped

1 ½ teaspoons light corn syrup

1 cup heavy cream

10 marshmallows, cut into quarters

½ cup lightly salted whole peanuts

½ cup chopped lightly salted peanuts

Preheat the oven to 300 degrees F. Butter the sides and bottom of a 9-by-13-inch baking pan or spray it with nonstick cooking spray.

In a large bowl, stir together the graham cracker crumbs and brown sugar. Add the butter. Use your hands to combine the mixture, then turn it out into the prepared pan. Using your hands, press the crust into an even layer along the bottom and up the sides of the pan. Use the bottom of a measuring cup to create a perfectly even crust.

Bake the crust for 10 to 15 minutes, or until the crust is golden brown. Remove the pan from the oven and place on a cooling rack.

In a large heatproof bowl, toss the chocolates together. Drizzle the corn syrup over the chocolate and set aside.

In a medium saucepan, bring the cream just to a boil. Remove from the heat and pour the cream over the chocolate mixture. Let stand for 2 to 3 minutes. Starting in the center of the bowl and working your way out to the edges, whisk the chocolate mixture in a circle until completely smooth. Fold in the marshmallows and the whole peanuts. Pour the mixture into the prepared pan and use an offset spatula to spread it as evenly as possible. Sprinkle the top with the chopped peanuts.

Refrigerate for at least 3 hours, or until set. Cut into squares and serve. The bars will keep in the refrigerator, tightly covered, for up to 3 days.

LEMON LIME BARS

CURD IS AN UGLY WORD FOR A DELICIOUS DESSERT. Made properly, curd is transformative, and can be used as a cake filling (as in our Lemon Drop Cake on page 63), as a simple spread for scones and toasts, or as a lovely tart filling. Our Lemon Lime Bars feature a tart and tangy curd with a smooth creamy consistency nestled up against the crunch of a crisp graham-coconut crust. This is a cooling summer dessert, but we love these bars so much we keep making them for weeks beyond the first cold snap.

YIELD: 24 BARS

BAKED NOTE

When you cover the bars with plastic wrap while chilling, be sure the plastic does not come in direct contact with the top of the bars, which will damage the look of the smooth curd layer. Use toothpicks inserted into the four corners of the bars to prop up the plastic.

FOR THE GRAHAM-COCONUT CRUST

1 cup sweetened shredded coconut
2 cups graham cracker crumbs (about 15-17 crackers)
2 tablespoons firmly packed light brown sugar
½ cup (1 stick) unsalted butter, melted

FOR THE LEMON LIME FILLING

11 large egg yolks
3 large eggs
1¾ cups sugar

¾ cup fresh lemon juice
2 tablespoons fresh lime juice
2 tablespoons grated lemon zest
2 tablespoons grated lime zest
¾ cup (1½ sticks) unsalted butter, softened and cut into 1-inch pieces
1/3 cup heavy cream

MAKE THE GRAHAM-COCONUT CRUST

Preheat the oven to 300 degrees F. Butter the sides and bottom of a 9-by-13-inch baking pan or spray it with nonstick cooking spray.

On a parchment-lined baking sheet, spread out the coconut. Put the baking sheet in the oven and toast the coconut until it starts to turn golden brown, 7 to 10 minutes. Remove from the oven, toss the coconut, and return it to the oven for 3 more minutes.

Put the graham cracker crumbs in a large bowl, add the toasted coconut and the brown sugar, and toss with your hands until combined. Add the melted butter. Use your hands to combine the mixture, then turn it out into the prepared pan. Using your hands, press the crust into an even layer on the bottom and up the sides of the pan. Use the bottom of a measuring cup to create a perfectly even crust.

Put the crust in the refrigerator for 15 minutes, then bake for 10 minutes, or until golden brown. Let the crust cool before adding the filling.

MAKE THE LEMON LIME FILLING

Increase the oven temperature to 325 degrees F.

Put the egg yolks, eggs, sugar, lemon and lime juices, and lemon and lime zests in a large, clean metal pot. Whisk until combined. Cook over medium heat, whisking constantly, until the mixture registers 180 degrees F. on a candy thermometer, about 10 minutes.

Remove from the heat and whisk in the butter and cream. Pour through a fine-mesh sieve directly into the cooled crust. Use a rubber spatula to press the curd through the sieve.

Make sure the curd is evenly distributed. Tap the pan gently against the counter to make a level layer.

Bake for 8 to 10 minutes, until the filling is just set. Transfer to a wire rack and let cool to room temperature. Wrap the pan in plastic (do not let the plastic touch the filling) and put it in the refrigerator for at least 2 hours. Cut into squares and serve.

The bars will keep in the refrigerator, tightly covered, for 2 days.

FRESHLY BAKED IDEA CUT AND PASTE

Cookie cutters aren't just for cookies anymore. Use your cookie cutters to create shapes out of brownies and bars.

Simply turn the brownies or bars out of the pan and onto a flat work surface. Dip the cookie cutter in hot water and press it into the brownie or bar mass. The brownie or bar may stick to the inside of the cookie cutter, but it should pop out easily with a little nudge. Place the brownie shapes on a platter, then use dyed white chocolate to pipe individual inscriptions or basic decorations. A small amount of melted chocolate acts as a good glue to adhere accents like sprinkles, M&Ms, nonpareils, gum drops, and chocolate chips.

And don't toss your scraps. You can place brownie or bar scraps in a food processor and pulse briefly to create a delicious topping for ice cream or cakes.

BAKED BARS

THE BAKED BAR IS AN EVERYTHING BAR—A KITCHEN-SINK EXTRAVAGANZA. The graham-coconut crust is the perfect support for layers of chocolate chips, walnuts, and condensed milk. You may have seen a version of this bar under a different name (Seven-Layer Bar, Hello Dolly Bar, Magic Bar), but our local version was influenced by our Brooklyn customers, who suggested adding white chocolate chunks and butterscotch chips. Crisp and gooey in all the right places, it's perfect in small portions.

YIELD: 24 BARS

BAKED NOTE

This really is an "anything goes" bar. You can replace the walnuts with any other nut, and you can feel free to leave out the white chocolate entirely. Our only suggestion is that you do not use milk chocolate chips instead of semisweet, as you need the darker chocolate to balance out the sweetness of the other ingredients.

FOR THE BAKED BAR CRUST

2 cups (about 6 ounces) sweetened shredded coconut

2½ cups finely ground graham cracker crumbs (about 20 crackers)

1 cup (2 sticks) unsalted butter, melted

FOR THE BAKED BAR FILLING

1⅓ cups walnut halves, toasted and chopped

1½ cups (9 ounces) semisweet chocolate chips

¾ cup white chocolate, coarsely chopped

¾ cup butterscotch chips

3¼ cups (26 ounces) sweetened condensed milk

MAKE THE BAKED BAR CRUST

Preheat the oven to 300 degrees F.

Butter the sides and bottom of a 9-by-13-inch baking pan or spray it with nonstick cooking spray.

On a parchment-lined baking sheet, spread out the coconut. Put the baking sheet in the oven and toast the coconut until it starts to turn golden brown, 7 to 10 minutes. Remove from the oven, toss the coconut, and return it to the oven for 3 more minutes.

Put the graham cracker crumbs in a large bowl, add the toasted coconut, and toss with your hands until combined. Add the butter. Use your hands to combine the mixture, then turn it out into the prepared pan. Using your hands, press the crust into an even layer on the bottom and up the sides of the pan. Use the bottom of a measuring cup to create a perfectly even crust.

Refrigerate the crust for 15 minutes, then bake for 10 minutes, or until golden brown. Transfer to a wire rack and let the crust cool completely.

Increase the oven temperature to 325 degrees F.

Evenly spread the nuts in the bottom of the crust.

Spread the chocolate chips over the walnuts, followed by the white chocolate, followed by the butterscotch chips.

In a steady stream, pour the sweetened condensed milk evenly over the filling. Shake the pan very gently to make sure the sweetened condensed milk is evenly distributed.

Bake for 30 to 40 minutes, rotating the pan every 10 minutes, until golden brown and bubbly. Transfer to a wire rack and let cool completely. Cut into squares and serve.

Baked Bars will keep, wrapped tightly and at room temperature, for up to 4 days.

MILLIONAIRE'S SHORTBREAD

THINK OF THIS BAR AS THE RICH MAN'S TWIX. Sheri Johnston, our good friend from Scotland, introduced us to two uniquely Scottish foods: haggis and millionaire's shortbread. Let's just say that we have no desire to revisit haggis, but we became addicted to her millionaire's shortbread. Deceptively simple, it consists of one layer of very good shortbread, one layer of thick caramel, and one layer of chocolate. Though all three elements are delicious in their own right, the beauty of this confection is that the whole truly ends up being greater than the sum of its parts.

YIELD: 24 BARS

BAKED NOTE

This is a messy bar. Crumbly shortbread, oozy caramel, and chocolate smudges abound. For cleaner edges, dip your knife in hot water and pat it dry before slicing. And make sure to serve the shortbread with lots of napkins.

FOR THE SHORTBREAD

½ cup sugar
1 ¼ cups (2½ sticks) unsalted butter, softened
2½ cups all-purpose flour
1 large egg yolk, slightly beaten

FOR THE CARAMEL FILLING

28 ounces sweetened condensed milk (two 14-ounce cans)

FOR THE CHOCOLATE GLAZE

6 ounces dark chocolate (60% cacao), coarsely chopped
1 teaspoon light corn syrup
½ cup (1 stick) unsalted butter, softened, cut into cubes

MAKE THE SHORTBREAD

Preheat the oven to 350 degrees F. Butter the bottom and sides of a 9-by-13-inch baking pan.

In the bowl of an electric mixer fitted with the paddle attachment, beat the sugar and butter together until blended.

Add 2 cups of the flour and beat until well combined. Add the egg yolk and beat for a few seconds, or until just combined.

Turn the dough out onto a lightly floured work surface. Dust the top of the dough and your hands with a little flour. Use your hands to gently work the dough into a 6-by-6-inch square. You will have to turn the dough and sprinkle the top with flour as you go. Sprinkle the remaining ½ cup flour on the surface of the dough. Fold the dough over and knead until incorporated, then flatten the dough into a rectangle. Transfer the rectangle to the prepared pan and press it into the pan.

Prick the dough all over with a fork and bake in the center of the oven for 20 to 22 minutes, until golden brown. Transfer to a wire rack and let cool completely.

MAKE THE CARAMEL FILLING

Stovetop method: Put the sweetened condensed milk in a medium heat-proof bowl and set it over a saucepan of boiling water over low heat. Cook for 1 to 1 ½ hours, until thick and caramel colored. Remove the bowl from the pan and beat until smooth.

Microwave oven method: Put the sweetened condensed milk in a large microwave-safe bowl. Cook on 50 percent power (medium) for 4 minutes, stirring briskly halfway through, until smooth. Cook on 30 percent power (medium-low) for 12 to 18 minutes, until very thick and caramel colored, stirring briskly every 2 minutes, until smooth.

Pour the caramel filling over the cooled shortbread and place the pan in the refrigerator until cool, about two hours.

MAKE THE CHOCOLATE GLAZE

In a large nonreactive metal bowl, combine the chocolate, corn syrup, and butter. Set the bowl over a saucepan of simmering water and cook, stirring with a rubber spatula, until the mixture is completely smooth. Remove the bowl from the pan and stir for 30 seconds to cool slightly. Pour the mixture over the chilled caramel layer and use an offset spatula to spread it into an even layer.

Put in the refrigerator for 1 hour, or until the glaze hardens.

Remove the pan from the refrigerator 30 minutes before serving so as not to crack the chocolate glaze. Cut into squares and serve.

The bars can be stored in the refrigerator, tightly covered, for up to 4 days.

HONEYCOMB BARS

YOU PROBABLY DIDN'T EVEN KNOW YOU NEEDED THIS BAR. Well, wait until you taste it. The honeycomb bar is not exactly common, nor does it have an immediately recognizable taste, but that's what makes this truly uncategorizable bar so wonderful. Almonds and dried cherries are encased in an orange-honey glaze and baked in a buttery sweet tart dough. We're convinced that these bars, equally delicious for breakfast or dessert, will become part of your permanent repertoire.

YIELD: 24 BARS

BAKED NOTE

Sweet tart dough freezes well. Make a double batch of the dough, wrap half of it tightly in a double layer of plastic wrap, and freeze it for future use.

FOR THE SWEET TART DOUGH

½ cup (1 stick) unsalted butter, softened
½ cup sugar
2 teaspoons heavy cream
1 large egg yolk
1 teaspoon pure vanilla extract
1½ cups all-purpose flour
Pinch of salt

FOR THE HONEYCOMB BAR FILLING

¾ cup dried cherries, chopped

⅓ cup diced candied orange peel (see page 28)
2 tablespoons cake flour
Pinch of salt
1⅓ cups sugar
1¼ cups heavy cream
⅓ cup honey
½ cup (1 stick) unsalted butter
Shot of brandy or bourbon
2½ cups sliced almonds, toasted

MAKE THE SWEET TART DOUGH

In the bowl of an electric mixer fitted with the paddle attachment, cream the butter and sugar until combined.

In a small bowl whisk together the heavy cream, egg yolk, and vanilla. Add this to the butter and sugar mixture and beat until incorporated. Scrape down the bowl and add the flour and salt until just combined.

Turn out the mixture onto a lightly floured surface and form into an oblong disk. Wrap the disk tightly in plastic and refrigerate for 30 minutes.

Preheat the oven to 350 degrees F. Butter the sides and bottom of a 9-by-13-inch glass or light-colored metal baking pan.

Roll out the dough into a large rectangle roughly the shape of the pan. Transfer the dough to the pan, and press into the bottom of the pan (do not press up the sides). Don't worry if you aren't able to roll out a perfect crust. The dough is quite forgiving and can be pressed, in pieces, into the pan by hand. Cover the dough with a sheet of parchment paper (see page 95). Place dried beans or pie weights over the dough and bake for 10 minutes. Remove the beans and parchment paper and bake for another 5 minutes. Transfer from the oven to a cooling rack. Keep the oven on while you make the filling.

In a medium bowl, toss together the dried cherries, orange peel, cake flour, and salt. Set aside.

In a large saucepan over medium heat, stir together the sugar, heavy cream, honey, and butter. Clip a candy thermometer to the side of the pan and bring the mixture to the soft ball stage, approximately 240 degrees F. Do not stir the mixture while it is coming to this stage.

Once the mixture reaches 240 degrees F., add the brandy and remove from the heat.

Fold the dry ingredients and the almonds into the hot sugar mixture and pour the mixture into the sweet tart crust. Spread the filling evenly, and smooth the top.

Bake for about 15 minutes or until the bar is golden and bubbly.

Remove from the oven and allow to cool completely before cutting.

Bars can be stored at room temperature, covered and sealed, for up to 4 days.

BREWER'S BLONDIES

UNLIKE ANY BLONDIE YOU'VE EVER TASTED, OUR BLONDIE IS ENRICHED WITH MALT POWDER AND CRUSHED MALT BALLS, GIVING IT A WARM BARLEY FLAVOR. At Baked, we work with a local brewery, Six Points Ale, to blend their brewer's malt with the milk chocolate that will eventually end up swirled into the Brewer's Blondies. Since most home bakers do not have access to brewer's malt, we adapted the recipe slightly. Though there is a vast difference between malted barley (brewer's malt) and the malted milk powder used here, this bar is still completely delicious.

YIELD: 24 BARS

2⅓ cups all-purpose flour
1½ teaspoons baking powder
1 teaspoon salt
2 tablespoons malted milk powder
14 tablespoons unsalted butter, softened, cut into 1-inch cubes
1¾ cups firmly packed dark brown sugar
2 large eggs

2 teaspoons pure vanilla extract
¾ cup malted milk balls (like Whoppers or Maltesers), coarsely chopped in a food processor
¾ cup (9 ounces) semisweet chocolate chips
¾ cup toasted walnuts, chopped
Vanilla ice cream, to serve

BAKED NOTE

For the ultimate snack, place one Brewer's Blondie on a microwave-safe dish and heat it on high for 15 seconds. Remove the blondie from the microwave oven and top it with one heaping scoop of vanilla ice cream. Let the warmth of the blondie melt the ice cream for a few moments, then serve immediately.

Preheat the oven to 350 degrees F. Butter the bottom and sides of a 9-by-13-inch baking pan.

In a medium bowl, whisk the flour, baking powder, salt, and malted milk powder together.

In the bowl of an electric mixer fitted with the paddle attachment, beat the butter and brown sugar on medium speed until completely combined. Scrape down the bowl, add the eggs and vanilla, and beat until combined.

Add the flour mixture in two batches and beat until just combined. Add the malted milk balls, chocolate chips, and walnuts and beat until just combined, about 10 seconds. The mixture will be thick. Turn the mixture out into the prepared pan and use an offset spatula to spread it evenly.

Bake in the center of the oven for 25 to 30 minutes, or until a toothpick inserted into the center of the blondie comes out clean.

Transfer to a wire rack and let cool for 20 minutes. These blondies taste delicious warm. Cut them into squares and serve with ice cream. They also taste great at room temperature. Once thoroughly cooled, cover tightly with plastic wrap and keep at room temperature for up to 3 days.

RASPBERRY CRUMB BREAKFAST BAR

THE RASPBERRY CRUMB BAR IS NOT TECHNICALLY A BREAKFAST SWEET. It's a bar, and bars (as we are all taught) are generally eaten in the afternoon or after dinner. This bar defies categorization. The crumb oat layers are thin and crisp, and the raspberry filling is gently sweetened, making it the perfect morning pastry. At the same time, it is the kind of bar you might crave as the antidote to an uninspired lunch or as a midnight snack. In short, you can eat this bar any time you please.

YIELD: 24 BARS

BAKED NOTE

We hope the title of the Raspberry Crumb Breakfast Bar is not misleading. The word "crumb" often alludes to the thick topping on a cakey breakfast treat, but this bar is actually more like a thin raspberry sandwich.

FOR THE CRUST AND CRUMB

1 ½ cups all-purpose flour

1 cup firmly packed dark brown sugar

1 ¼ cups rolled oats

¾ teaspoon salt

¾ teaspoon baking powder

½ teaspoon baking soda

½ teaspoon cinnamon

¾ cup (1 ½ sticks) unsalted butter, cut into 1-inch pieces

FOR THE RASPBERRY FILLING

¼ cup firmly packed dark brown sugar

1 tablespoon grated lemon zest

½ teaspoon cinnamon

2 tablespoons all-purpose flour

1 pound raspberries, fresh or frozen

¼ cup fresh lemon juice

2 tablespoons unsalted butter, melted and cooled

MAKE THE CRUST AND CRUMB

Preheat the oven to 350 degrees F. Butter the bottom and sides of a 9-by-13-inch glass or light-colored metal baking pan. Put a long piece of parchment paper in the bottom of the pan, letting the parchment extend up the two short sides of the pan and overhang slightly on both ends. (This will make it easy to remove the bars from the pan after they have baked.) Butter the parchment.

Put the flour, brown sugar, oats, salt, baking powder, baking soda, and cinnamon in a food processor. Pulse in short bursts until combined. Add the butter and pulse until loose crumbs form.

Reserve 1 cup of the mixture and set aside. Pour the rest of the mixture into the prepared pan and use your hands or the back of a large wooden spoon to push the crust into an even layer in the bottom of the pan. The crust should touch the sides of the pan. Bake until golden brown, 12 to 15 minutes. Transfer to a wire rack and let the crust cool. Keep the oven on while you make the raspberry filling.

MAKE THE RASPBERRY FILLING

In a medium bowl, whisk the sugar, lemon zest, cinnamon, and flour together.

Add the raspberries, lemon juice, and butter and use your hands to toss gently until the raspberries are evenly coated.

ASSEMBLE AND BAKE THE BARS

Spread the raspberry filling evenly on top of the cooled crust. Sprinkle the reserved 1 cup crust mixture evenly on top of the filling.

Bake for 35 to 40 minutes, rotating the pan every 15 minutes, until the top is golden brown and the filling starts to bubble around the edges.

Transfer to a wire rack to cool completely, then cut into squares and serve. The bars can be stored in the refrigerator in an airtight container for up to 2 days.

PEANUT BUTTER CRISPY BARS

THIS IS, HANDS DOWN, THE MOST POPULAR REFRIGERATED BAR WE MAKE AT THE BAKERY. Essentially, this is a very grown-up and very decadent Rice Krispy Treat. The "crispys" are candied, then layered with a generous amount of peanut butter milk chocolate and topped with a glossy dark chocolate icing. We adapted this recipe from the very talented chef and chocolatier Andrew Shotts, who makes the most amazing chocolate truffles for his company, Garrison Confections.

YIELD: 9 BARS

BAKED NOTE

This dessert is extremely rich and best served in small portions (hence the small pan); however, the recipe can be easily doubled or tripled for larger parties.

FOR THE CRISPY CRUST

1¾ cups crisped rice cereal
¼ cup sugar
3 tablespoons light corn syrup
3 tablespoons unsalted butter, melted

FOR THE MILK CHOCOLATE PEANUT BUTTER LAYER

5 ounces good-quality milk chocolate, coarsely chopped
1 cup creamy peanut butter

FOR THE CHOCOLATE ICING

3 ounces dark chocolate (60 to 72% cacao), coarsely chopped
½ teaspoon light corn syrup
4 tablespoons (½ stick) unsalted butter

MAKE THE CRISPY CRUST

Lightly spray a paper towel with nonstick cooking spray and use it to rub the bottom and sides of an 8-inch square baking pan.

Put the cereal in a large bowl and set aside.

Pour ¼ cup water into a small saucepan. Gently add the sugar and corn syrup (do not let any sugar or syrup get on the sides of the pan) and use a small wooden spoon to stir the mixture until just combined. Put a candy thermometer in the saucepan. Cook over medium-high heat and bring to a boil; cook until the mixture reaches the soft ball stage, 235 degrees F.

Remove from the heat, stir in the butter, and pour the mixture over the cereal. Working quickly, stir until the cereal is thoroughly coated, then pour it into the prepared pan. Using your hands, press the mixture into the bottom of the pan (do not press up the sides). Let the crust cool to room temperature while you make the next layer.

MAKE THE MILK CHOCOLATE PEANUT BUTTER LAYER

In a large nonreactive metal bowl, stir together the chocolate and the peanut butter.

Set the bowl over a saucepan of simmering water and cook, stirring with a rubber spatula, until the mixture is smooth. Remove the bowl from the pan and stir for about 30 seconds to cool slightly. Pour the mixture over the cooled crust. Put the pan in the refrigerator for 1 hour, or until the top layer hardens.

MAKE THE CHOCOLATE ICING

In a large nonreactive metal bowl, combine the chocolate, corn syrup, and butter.

Set the bowl over a saucepan of simmering water and cook, stirring with a rubber spatula, until the mixture is completely smooth. Remove the bowl from the pan and stir for 30 seconds to cool slightly. Pour the mixture over the chilled milk chocolate peanut butter layer and spread into an even layer. Put the pan in the refrigerator for 1 hour or until the topping hardens.

Cut into 9 squares and serve. The bars can be stored in the refrigerator, covered tightly, for up to 4 days.

FRESHLY BAKED IDEA THE CANDY STORE

Small kitchen? Need space? Use a tackle box or empty toolbox to store and organize less frequently used (but ever so important) candy and baking supplies. A basic toolbox should contain a candy thermometer, laminated instruction cards for "How to Temper Chocolate" and "Understanding Your Candy Thermometer," a small ruler (for aid in cutting bars, brownies, and marshmallows), and perhaps some of your favorite coloring gels. You can also use your toolbox to store and organize an extra set of measuring spoons, a Microplane grater, and pretty much anything else you would need for candy and chocolate making.

The cookie is king in our kitchen. Often we find ourselves buried deep in a sea of dirty pots and pans, sweating over the fine details of a delicate cake, or cursing a particular pie dough, and we wonder why we didn't just make a batch of cookies instead.

Most cookies are exceptionally easy to make. Just one or two bowls, a few basic ingredients, a quick mix, and your dough is finished. Though perhaps not as visually elegant as some other baked goods, cookies can be so satisfying. Serve them slightly warm, arranged on a large white platter with the requisite glass of cold milk (served in an old-fashioned tumbler, of course), and cookies can be just as five-star as any other dessert.

Our selection of recipes celebrates all types of cookies. We've included old-school champs like our ultimate peanut butter cookies (page 140), studded with milk chocolate chunks, and a new take on the whoopie pie, our Pumpkin Whoopie Pies with Cream Cheese Filling (page 151). We've also included a cookie for the chocolate obsessed: the Black Forest (page 142), a dark and rich cookie loaded with cherries and white chocolate chips. These recipes have been with us forever, and we know they will become part of your baking repertoire.

Cookie dough is very accommodating. Feel free to replace additions like nuts, chocolate chunks, or candies, or leave them out altogether. We also recommend a baking-on-demand philosophy when it comes to cookies: Bake only as many cookies as you plan to serve right away, and keep the extra dough on hand, in the fridge, for another occasion. (Most of the doughs here will keep, tightly covered and refrigerated, for up to 5 days.) This ensures that the cookies you serve are always fresh and, better yet, warm.

Finally, as a last bit of cookie wisdom, we encourage you to treat your cookies with the respect you would give any other dessert. Use the same dark, rich cocoa powder and chocolate you would afford any delicate truffle, and make sure your butter and eggs are the right temperature. Oh, and don't overmix. Treat your cookie right, and the results will leave you speechless.

CHOCOLATE CHIP COOKIES

IT'S EASY TO MAKE A DELICIOUS CHOCOLATE CHIP COOKIE. You should never settle for the tasteless, chalky, lazy versions found in quickie marts and at mass-market kiosks. A good chocolate chip cookie, in our opinion, is one of life's small pleasures, and you should treat it as such. Pay special attention to your ingredients. Use a high-grade butter (experiment with some of the specialty butters on the market), fresh eggs, and real vanilla. This recipe produces our favorite type of chocolate chip cookie: slightly crisp edges and a soft center. We couldn't help ourselves with the chocolate, so we also added more chips than usual to the batter.

YIELD: 24 COOKIES

2 cups all-purpose flour
1 teaspoon salt
1 teaspoon baking soda
1 cup (2 sticks) unsalted butter, softened
1 cup firmly packed dark brown sugar

½ cup granulated sugar
2 large eggs
2 teaspoons pure vanilla extract
2 ⅔ cups (16 ounces) semisweet
    chocolate chips

BAKED NOTE

You can leave the dough, tightly covered, in your refrigerator for up to 5 days and bake it off in small batches so you can have warm, fresh-from-the-oven cookies any time you like.

In a large bowl, whisk the flour, salt, and baking soda together and set aside.

In the bowl of an electric mixer fitted with the paddle attachment, beat the butter and sugars together until smooth and creamy. Scrape down the bowl and add the eggs, one at a time, beating until each is incorporated. The mixture will look light and fluffy. Add the vanilla and beat for 5 seconds.

Add half of the flour mixture and mix for 15 seconds. Add the remaining flour mixture and beat until just incorporated.

Using a spatula or wooden spoon, fold in the chocolate chips.

Cover the bowl tightly and put in the refrigerator for 6 hours.

Preheat the oven to 375 degrees F. Line two baking sheets with parchment paper.

Use an ice cream scoop with a release mechanism to scoop out dough in 2-tablespoon-size balls. Use your hands to shape the dough into perfect balls and place them on the prepared baking sheets, about 1 inch apart. Bake for 12 to 14 minutes, rotating the pans once during the cooking time, until the edges of the cookies are golden brown and the tops just start to darken.

Remove the pan from the oven and cool on a wire rack for 5 minutes. Use a spatula to transfer the individual cookies to the rack to cool completely (although they are delicious warm).

The cookies can be stored in an airtight container for up to 3 days.

PEANUT BUTTER COOKIES WITH MILK CHOCOLATE CHUNKS

THIS IS NOT YOUR ORDINARY PEANUT BUTTER COOKIE. It is, in our humble opinion, the *only* peanut butter cookie. Our cookie is neither too dry and crumbly, nor too moist and characterless; rather, it is the perfect balance of crispy and chewy. But the burst of old-school peanut butter flavor and huge milk chocolate chunks is what really puts this cookie in its own league. It is the type of cookie you will have to hide or lock down if you want it to remain in your cookie jar for more than a few hours.

YIELD: 24 COOKIES

BAKED NOTE

We know there may be some temptation to replace the milk chocolate chunks with semisweet chocolate chips, but don't give in. Semisweet chips taste almost bitter against the peanut butter, while the milk chocolate is a natural and delightful combo.

1¾ cups all-purpose flour
2 teaspoons baking soda
1 teaspoon salt
1 cup (2 sticks) unsalted butter, softened, cut into 1-inch pieces
1 cup granulated sugar, plus more for sprinkling

1 cup firmly packed dark brown sugar
2 large eggs
1 teaspoon pure vanilla extract
1 cup creamy peanut butter
6 ounces good milk chocolate, coarsely chopped

Sift the flour, baking soda, and salt into a medium bowl and set aside.

In the bowl of an electric mixer fitted with the paddle attachment, beat the butter and sugars together until fluffy. Scrape down the bowl and add the eggs, one at a time, beating until each is incorporated. The mixture will look light and fluffy. Add the vanilla and peanut butter and beat until just incorporated.

Add half of the flour mixture and mix for 15 seconds. Add the remaining flour mixture and mix until just incorporated.

Using a spatula or wooden spoon, fold in the chocolate. Cover the bowl tightly and refrigerate for at least 3 hours.

Preheat the oven to 375 degrees F. Line two baking sheets with parchment paper.

Drop the dough by rounded tablespoons onto the prepared baking sheets, at least 2 inches apart. With the palm of your hand, very gently press each cookie down so it forms a very tall disk shape. *Do not press too hard* and *do not press it flat.*

Sprinkle the tops of the cookies with granulated sugar and bake for 10 to 12 minutes, rotating the pan halfway through the baking time, until the tops of the cookies just begin to brown.

Remove the pan from the oven and cool on a wire rack for 5 minutes. Use a spatula to transfer the individual cookies to the rack to cool completely (although they are also delicious warm).

The cookies can be stored, in an airtight container, for up to 3 days.

FRESHLY BAKED IDEA THE LOVE LOG

Give the gift of love. Or at least the gift of cookies. This is an easy, likable host or hostess gift.

Make your favorite cookie dough. Chill it for about 2 hours to firm it up slightly. Scoop the dough out onto a sheet of parchment paper and shape it into the form of a log, leaving at least four inches of paper on either end of the dough. Roll the dough up in the parchment so it is completely covered. Use twine or ribbon to tie either end of the parchment (it should look like a giant Tootsie Roll). Attach a handwritten card with baking instructions and store it in your refrigerator until you are ready to give your log.

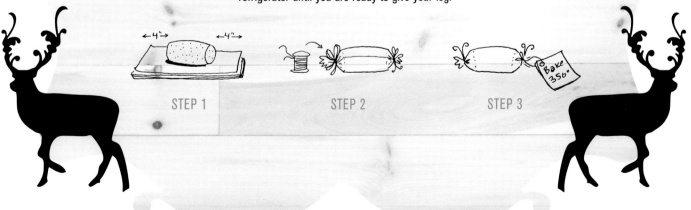

STEP 1   STEP 2   STEP 3

BLACK FOREST CHOCOLATE COOKIES

BLACK FOREST CAKE IS A CLASSIC GERMAN DESSERT, OFTEN POORLY TRANSLATED IN AMERICA INTO A LUMPY MESS OF DRY CHOCOLATE CAKE, SUPER-SWEET CHERRY PRESERVES, AND CANNED WHIPPED CREAM. A proper version of the cake includes chocolate cake layers, soaked in kirsch (cherry liqueur), lightly sweetened cherries, and freshly whipped cream. We interpreted the classic but kitschy cake with the utmost respect. Our Black Forest cookie is a very rich chocolate cookie tempered with a smattering of dried cherries and white chocolate chips. They are best served warm, with a slightly gooey center.

YIELD: 24 COOKIES

¾ cup all-purpose flour
1 teaspoon baking powder
½ teaspoon salt
16 ounces dark chocolate (60 to 72% cacao), coarsely chopped
10 tablespoons unsalted butter, cut into 1-inch pieces
6 large eggs

1¼ cups granulated sugar
1 cup firmly packed light brown sugar
1 tablespoon pure vanilla extract
1 cup (6 ounces) semisweet chocolate chips
1 cup (6 ounces) white chocolate chips
1 cup (6 ounces) dried cherries

BAKED NOTE

The dried cherries are delicious in this cookie, but if you have a true, die-hard chocolate fan in your life, you can replace the dried cherries and white chocolate chips with regular semisweet chocolate chips.

Sift the flour, baking powder, and salt together into a medium bowl and set aside.

In a large nonreactive metal bowl, combine the dark chocolate and butter. Set the bowl over a saucepan of simmering water and cook, stirring with a rubber spatula, until the chocolate and butter are completely melted and the mixture is smooth. Set aside to cool.

In the bowl of an electric mixer fitted with the whisk attachment, beat the eggs and sugars on high speed until the mixture is pale and thick, about 5 minutes.

Add the cooled chocolate mixture and the vanilla and beat until just combined. Scrape down the bowl and beat again for 10 seconds.

Add the flour mixture and mix on low until just combined, about 10 seconds. Do not overmix.

Using a spatula or wooden spoon, fold in the chocolate chips, white chocolate chips, and dried cherries. The dough will look very loose, but it will harden in the refrigerator. Refrigerate for 6 hours or overnight.

Preheat the oven to 375 degrees F. Line two baking sheets with parchment paper.

Drop the dough by rounded tablespoons onto the prepared baking sheets, about 1 inch apart. Bake for 10 to 12 minutes, rotating the pans halfway through the baking time, until the tops of the cookies are set and begin to show a few cracks. Remove from the oven and let cool slightly before removing from the pans and serving.

The cookies can be stored in an airtight container for up to 3 days.

MONSTER COOKIES

THIS COOKIE IS THE FRANKENSTEIN'S MONSTER OF THE COOKIE WORLD. One part oatmeal cookie, one part peanut butter cookie, and one part chocolate chip cookie, it is many things to many people. We re-created this rather large, chewy cookie as an homage to the Monster Cookies we remember eating in grade school, only our version is slightly less sweet and a whole lot better. Don't leave out the corn syrup—it's integral for the cookie.

YIELD: 36 COOKIES

BAKED NOTE

At the bakery, we buy orange M&Ms in bulk for this cookie, as it is a favorite color of ours. If you want to purchase M&Ms in your favorite color, visit www.m-ms.com.

½ cup all-purpose flour
1 tablespoon baking soda
Pinch of salt
5¾ cups rolled oats
¾ cup (1½ sticks) cold unsalted butter, cut into cubes
1½ cups firmly packed light brown sugar
1½ cups granulated sugar

5 large eggs
¼ teaspoon light corn syrup
¼ teaspoon pure vanilla extract
2 cups creamy peanut butter
1 cup (6 ounces) semisweet chocolate chips
1 cup (6 ounces) M&Ms

In a large bowl, whisk the flour, baking soda, and salt together. Add the oats and stir until the ingredients are evenly combined.

In the bowl of an electric mixer fitted with the paddle attachment, cream the butter until smooth and pale in color. Add the sugars and mix on low speed until just incorporated. Do not overmix.

Scrape down the bowl and add the eggs, one at a time, beating until smooth (about 20 seconds) and scraping down the bowl after each addition. Add the corn syrup and vanilla and beat until just incorporated.

Scrape down the bowl and add the peanut butter. Mix on low speed until just combined. Add the oat mixture in three additions, mixing on low speed until just incorporated.

Use a spatula or wooden spoon to fold in the chocolate chips and M&Ms. Cover the bowl tightly and refrigerate for 5 hours.

Preheat the oven to 375 degrees F. Line two baking sheets with parchment paper.

Use an ice cream scoop with a release mechanism to scoop out the dough in 2-tablespoon-size balls onto the prepared baking sheets, 2 inches apart. Bake for 12 to 15 minutes, rotating the pans halfway through the baking time, until the cookies just begin to brown. Let cool on the pans for 8 to 10 minutes before transferring the cookies to a wire rack to cool completely. Cookies can be stored in an airtight container for up to 3 days.

OATMEAL CHERRY NUT COOKIES

SOMETIMES EVEN THE MOST LOVED COOKIE NEEDS AN UPDATE. We adore traditional oatmeal cookies, but decided to reinterpret the standard recipe with a hint of winter spices, and we ditched the raisins entirely. Dried cherries, tangy and chewy, are unexpectedly delicious here. These cookies are moist on the inside with a crunchy exterior, perfect for dipping in hot chocolate or cold milk.

YIELD: 36 COOKIES

1½ cups all-purpose flour
1 teaspoon baking soda
1 teaspoon salt
2 teaspoons cinnamon
1 teaspoon freshly grated nutmeg
¼ teaspoon ground cardamom
1 cup (2 sticks) unsalted butter, softened
1¼ cups firmly packed dark brown sugar

¼ cup granulated sugar
2 large eggs
1 teaspoon pure vanilla extract
2¾ cups rolled oats
1 cup (8 ounces) dried cherries
½ cup (4 ounces) chopped toasted walnuts

BAKED NOTE

If you bake and cook often, you should buy whole nutmeg and grate it fresh for each use. Freshly grated nutmeg is wonderfully aromatic, and will give your whole kitchen a warm, homey scent.

In a large bowl, whisk the flour, baking soda, salt, cinnamon, nutmeg, and cardamom together and set aside.

In the bowl of an electric mixer fitted with the paddle attachment, beat the butter and sugars together on medium-high speed until smooth and creamy. Scrape down the bowl and add the eggs, one at a time, beating until each is incorporated. Add the vanilla and beat for 5 seconds.

Add half of the flour mixture and mix for 15 seconds. Add the remaining flour mixture and beat until just incorporated. Scrape down the bowl, add the oats, and beat until just combined. Use a spatula or wooden spoon to fold in the cherries and walnuts.

Cover the bowl tightly and refrigerate for 6 hours.

Preheat the oven to 375 degrees F. Line two baking sheets with parchment paper.

Drop the dough by rounded tablespoons onto the prepared baking sheets. With the palm of your hand, gently press each cookie down so it forms a tall disk shape. *Do not* press too hard and *do not* press it flat. Bake for 12 to 14 minutes, rotating the pans halfway through the baking time, until the cookies just begin to brown.

Remove the pan from the oven and cool on a wire rack for 5 minutes. Use a spatula to transfer the individual cookies to the rack to cool completely (although they are also delicious warm). The cookies can be stored, in an airtight container, for up to 3 days.

HAZELNUT CINNAMON CHIP BISCOTTI

TRADITIONS RUN STRONG IN ITALIAN FAMILIES. We are descendants of strong-willed Italian grandmothers who are absolutely, positively certain that almond biscotti are the only biscotti. While we adore Italian grandmothers and almond biscotti, we are, by nature, nontraditionalist. Our biscotti are firm, full of hazelnuts, always dunked in coffee, and larger than Grandma would approve of.

YIELD: 24 LARGE BISCOTTI

1⅓ cups sugar
1¼ teaspoons baking powder
1¼ teaspoons salt
1 teaspoon cinnamon
4 large eggs
2 teaspoons pure vanilla extract

3¼ cups all-purpose flour
1½ cups blanched hazelnuts, toasted
1¾ cups (10 ounces) semisweet chocolate chips
1 large egg white

BAKED NOTE

If you enjoy making biscotti on a regular basis, you may wish to invest in a dough scraper (or bench knife). This inexpensive tool is great for shaping and cutting any type of dough.

Preheat the oven to 350 degrees F. Line a baking sheet with parchment paper.

In a small bowl, whisk together the sugar, baking powder, salt, and cinnamon.

In the bowl of an electric mixer fitted with the paddle attachment, beat the eggs and the sugar mixture together until the color is uniform and the mixture is thick. Add the vanilla and beat for 5 seconds. Add the flour in two batches and beat until just combined. Scrape down the bowl and mix for a few seconds more. Add the hazelnuts and chocolate chips and beat until just combined.

Turn the dough out onto the prepared baking sheet and shape it into a log about 16 inches long, 3½ inches wide, and ¾ inch thick. Use an offset spatula to smooth the surface of the dough. Bake for 20 to 25 minutes until firm, but not browned. Let cool on the pan for 10 minutes.

Lower the oven temperature to 325 degrees F.

While the log is cooling, whisk the egg white and 2 tablespoons water together and use a pastry brush to brush the egg wash onto the top of the log.

Cut the log into ¾-inch slices with a serrated knife, set them on the baking sheet cut sides up and down, and bake for 25 minutes. Remove the pan from the oven and cool on a wire rack for 5 minutes. Use a spatula to transfer the individual biscotti to a rack to cool completely. The biscotti will keep in an airtight container for up to 2 weeks.

 **PISTACHIO CHERRY BISCOTTI**

Omit the cinnamon, replace the hazelnuts with 1 cup pistachios, and replace the chocolate chips with 1 cup dried cherries.

CLASSIC SUGAR COOKIES

THE HUMBLE SUGAR COOKIE DOESN'T OFTEN GET ITS DUE. Too often it's coated in bright garish icing and is inedibly sweet. Our recipe delivers a simple, chewy cookie that's the perfect canvas for our favorite minimal, almost stark, decoration. A bright, white sugar cookie with a few colorful accents really makes a statement when compared with the color overload of most sugar cookies.

YIELD: 15–18 2½ INCH COOKIES

BAKED NOTE

If you are traveling with sugar cookies or mailing them, make sure to place a sheet of waxed paper or parchment paper between the cookies. Even though your cookies may appear completely dry, they can smear or stick to other cookies during transit.

FOR THE CLASSIC SUGAR COOKIES

1¾ cups all-purpose flour
¼ teaspoon salt
¼ teaspoon baking powder
¾ cups (1½ sticks) unsalted butter, softened
2 tablespoons cold vegetable shortening
⅔ cup sugar
1 large egg
1 teaspoon pure vanilla extract

FOR THE BASIC ROYAL ICING

2 cups confectioners' sugar, sifted
2 large egg whites
2 teaspoons freshly squeezed lemon juice

MAKE THE CLASSIC SUGAR COOKIES

In a medium bowl, whisk together the flour, salt, and baking powder and set aside.

In the bowl of an electric mixer fitted with the paddle attachment, beat the butter, shortening, and sugar together until light and fluffy. Add the egg and vanilla and beat until just combined. Add the flour mixture and mix until incorporated. Wrap the dough in plastic and refrigerate for at least 4 hours.

Preheat the oven to 325 degrees F. Line two baking sheets with parchment paper.

Dust a work surface with a sprinkling of flour. Unwrap the chilled dough, and put it directly on the work surface. Roll the dough ¼ inch thick. Use your favorite cookie cutter to cut shapes in the dough, and transfer the cookies to the prepared baking sheets.

Bake the cookies for 12 minutes, until they are set but not browned. Remove from the oven and place the baking sheet on a cooling rack for 5 minutes. Use a spatula to transfer the cookies to the rack to cool completely.

MAKE THE BASIC ROYAL ICING

In a large bowl, whisk together the sugar, egg whites, and lemon juice until the mixture is completely smooth. The mixture should have the texture of a

glaze. If the mixture is too thin, add a bit more sugar. If the mixture is too thick, add a few drops of lemon juice. You can add a few drops of food coloring if desired, or you can divide the icing among many mixing bowls if you need more than one color.

The best way to ice sugar cookies is with a pastry bag fitted with a small or medium tip. First, outline the cookie or design, then fill it in. Let the icing harden before serving.

The cookies can be kept in an airtight container for up to 3 days.

PUMPKIN WHOOPIE PIES WITH CREAM CHEESE FILLING

TRY AS WE MIGHT, WE WERE NEVER HUGE FANS OF THE TRADITIONAL WHOOPIE PIE. We love the concept of two cakey chocolate cookies with a fair amount of cream sandwiched between them, but every execution we tried was always less than desirable. Maybe it was the cream filling with the shortening aftertaste. Maybe it was the too-wet cookie itself. After all, there is such a thing as being too moist. So we took some liberties with the whoopie pie and created our own version, which was named one of the top 100 tastes of 2007 by *Time Out New York*. Our Pumpkin Whoopie Pie makes the perfect midnight snack, with its soft, cakelike cookie and chilled cream cheese filling. For bite-sized pies, use a melon baller to scoop the dough.

YIELD: 12 WHOOPIE PIES

BAKED NOTE

Make sure you chill the pumpkin puree thoroughly before making this recipe. The chilled puree will make your whoopies easier to scoop and give them a domed top.

FOR THE PUMPKIN WHOOPIE COOKIES

3 cups all-purpose flour
1 teaspoon salt
1 teaspoon baking powder
1 teaspoon baking soda
2 tablespoons cinnamon
1 tablespoon ginger
1 tablespoon cloves
2 cups firmly packed dark brown sugar
1 cup vegetable oil
3 cups chilled pumpkin puree
2 large eggs
1 teaspoon pure vanilla extract

FOR THE CREAM CHEESE FILLING

3 cups confectioners' sugar
½ cup (1 stick) unsalted butter, softened
8 ounces cream cheese, softened
1 teaspoon pure vanilla extract

MAKE THE PUMPKIN WHOOPIE COOKIES

Preheat the oven to 350 degrees F. Line two baking sheets with parchment paper.

In a large bowl, whisk the flour, salt, baking powder, baking soda, cinnamon, ginger, and cloves together and set aside.

In a separate bowl, whisk the brown sugar and oil together until combined. Add the pumpkin puree and whisk to combine thoroughly. Add the eggs and vanilla and whisk until combined.

Sprinkle the flour mixture over the pumpkin mixture and whisk until completely combined.

Use a small ice cream scoop with a release mechanism to drop heaping tablespoons of the dough onto the prepared baking sheets, about 1 inch apart. Bake for 10 to 12 minutes, until the cookies are just starting to crack on top and a toothpick inserted into the center of a cookie comes out clean. Remove from the oven and let the cookies cool completely on the pan while you make the filling.

MAKE THE CREAM CHEESE FILLING

Sift the confectioners' sugar into a medium bowl and set aside.

In the bowl of an electric mixer fitted with the paddle attachment, beat the butter until it is completely smooth, with no visible lumps. Add the cream cheese and beat until combined.

Add the confectioners' sugar and vanilla and beat until smooth. Be careful not to overbeat the filling, or it will lose structure. (The filling can be made 1 day ahead. Cover the bowl tightly and put it in the refrigerator. Let the filling soften at room temperature before using.)

ASSEMBLE THE WHOOPIE PIES

Turn half of the cooled cookies upside down (flat side facing up).

Use an ice cream scoop or a tablespoon to drop a large dollop of filling onto the flat side of the cookie. Place another cookie, flat side down, on top of the filling. Press down slightly so that the filling spreads to the edges of the cookie. Repeat until all the cookies are used. Put the whoopie pies in the refrigerator for about 30 minutes to firm up before serving.

The whoopie pies will keep for up to 3 days, on a parchment-lined baking sheet covered with plastic wrap, in the refrigerator.

FRESHLY BAKED IDEA THE COOKIE SWAP

Impress your friends and family with a great party and a personalized cookie cookbook.
THE CONCEPT Have a party, enjoy a multitude of cookies, and create a keepsake album of everyone's favorite cookies and their accompanying recipes.

STEP 1 Invite your friends and family to a "Cookie Swap" party, with the only requirement being that each person bring one batch of his or her favorite cookies, and the recipe. As host, you provide a few cookie recipes of your own, refreshments, and take-home boxes.

STEP 2 Over the course of the party, make sure to photograph each cookie with a digital camera. Don't forget to take some candid shots of the guests as well. Trade cookies, recipe tips, and cookie anecdotes during the party. Should there be any leftovers, make sure each guest is given a box of assorted cookies for future snacking.

STEP 3 At some point over the following few days, enter each of the recipes into a word processing program, and add the contributor's name to each recipe. Sprinkle helpful hints and tips throughout and make sure that your recipe writing style is consistent and clear.

STEP 4 Upload your photos from the party and use an online digital photo service to add the images to an online album. Many online photo sites also offer the ability to create physical photo albums (for a modest fee). Create an album with a photograph of each cookie on a left-hand page and the corresponding recipe on the opposite page. Make sure to add those candid shots you took, so guests will remember all the fun they had! Order albums for the party's guests and have them mailed directly to their homes.

BAKED TRICOLOR COOKIES

THE TRICOLOR COOKIE, OR RAINBOW COOKIE, IS A NEARLY UBIQUITOUS PART OF THE TRADITIONAL AMERICAN-ITALIAN DESSERT PLATTER, AND IT HAPPENS TO BE RENATO'S FAVORITE SNACK. Our version of the cookie incorporates our bakery's colors (brown, white, and orange) instead of the red, white, and green used to evoke the Italian flag in the original cookie. We've also tweaked the amounts of marzipan and added some orange zest for a citrus zing. The layers are sandwiched together with an apricot-amaretto jam and topped off with a glossy dark chocolate glaze for a modern spin on an old-school classic.

YIELD: 20 COOKIES

BAKED NOTE

Customize your tri-color cookies by using different colors of food coloring. Remember that coloring the chocolate layer will prove unsuccessful.

FOR THE COOKIE LAYERS

1 cup all-purpose flour
¼ teaspoon salt
7 ounces almond paste (recipe follows)
¾ cup sugar
½ teaspoon pure almond extract
¾ cup (1½ sticks) unsalted butter, softened
3 large eggs
Grated zest of 1 orange
Orange food coloring (liquid or gel)
2 tablespoons dark unsweetened cocoa powder, sifted

FOR THE FILLING

⅔ cup apricot jam
2 tablespoons amaretto liqueur

FOR THE GLAZE

6 ounces dark chocolate (60% cacao), coarsely chopped
1 teaspoon light corn syrup
½ cup (1 stick) unsalted butter, softened, cut into cubes

MAKE THE COOKIE LAYERS

Preheat the oven to 350 degrees F. Butter three 8-inch square baking pans. Line the bottom of each pan with parchment paper and butter the parchment. Dust with flour and knock out the excess flour.

Sift the flour and salt together in a small bowl and set aside.

In the bowl of an electric mixer fitted with the paddle attachment, beat the almond paste, sugar, and almond extract together until small crumbs form. Add the butter and beat on high speed until the mixture is combined. Scrape down the bowl and add the eggs, one at a time, beating until each is incorporated. Add the orange zest and beat until combined. Add the flour mixture in three parts, beating on low speed after each additon until combined.

Divide the batter among three small mixing bowls.

In the first bowl, add a few drops of orange food coloring to the batter, and

mix well. Continue to add a few drops of food coloring and mixing until the batter is medium orange in color.

In the second bowl, add the cocoa powder to the batter and whisk until fully incorporated.

Leave the third bowl plain.

Pour each batter into a prepared pan and smooth the tops. Bake the layers for 12 to 15 minutes or until a toothpick inserted in the center of each layer comes out clean.

Transfer the pans to a wire rack and cool for 20 minutes. Invert the cakes onto the rack, remove the pans, and let cool completely. Remove the parchment.

MAKE THE FILLING

In a small saucepan over low heat, stir the jam and amaretto until warmed through and completely blended, 3 to 5 minutes.

ASSEMBLE THE TRICOLOR COOKIES

Place the chocolate layer on a serving rack and evenly spread half of the apricot jam over the top. Top with the plain (or white) layer and spread with the remaining apricot filling. Top with the orange layer and let the layers sit in the refrigerator for 5 minutes (or while you make the chocolate glaze).

MAKE THE GLAZE

In a large nonreactive metal bowl, combine the chocolate, corn syrup, and butter. Set the bowl over a saucepan of simmering water and cook, stirring with a rubber spatula, until the mixture is completely smooth. Remove the bowl from the pan and stir for 30 seconds to cool slightly.

Spread the glaze over the top of the bar cookies, completely covering the orange layer (some glaze may spill down the sides of the cake). Place the tray in the refrigerator until the chocolate topping completely sets (about 1 hour). Remove the tray from the refrigerator, wait 30 minutes for the chocolate to warm up, and cut into 20 individual squares or use a small cookie cutter to create your own shapes.

The bars can be stored in the refrigerator, tightly covered, for up to 4 days.

HOW TO MAKE ALMOND PASTE

1½ cups finely ground almonds
1 cup confectioners' sugar, sifted
½ teaspoon pure almond extract

Put all the ingredients in a food processor with 2 tablespoons water and process until a paste forms. Remove from the food processor, wrap tightly in plastic, and refrigerate until ready to use. Extra almond paste, tightly wrapped, keeps well in the freezer.

7

CHOCOLATES, CANDIES & CONFECTIONS

It all started with the marshmallow.

Our thinking at the bakery was such: If you serve hot chocolate, you have to serve marshmallows. And if you serve marshmallows, you have to make them yourself, because a store-bought marshmallow is, well, just awful. So we set about making our own marshmallows.

At first, our marshmallow project was merely for the hot chocolate drinkers. We would produce a small tray of vanilla marshmallows at the end of a long day of baking and hope that we would sell enough hot chocolates topped with marshmallows the next day to make the endeavor worthwhile. But soon, customers started ordering marshmallows even if they weren't ordering hot chocolate. Then they started requesting more flavors. Then they started ordering them in mass quantities. You could say that the marshmallows started to take over the bakery.

Today, the Baked marshmallows are rock stars. They are featured prominently on the Baked counter in an array of flavors—vanilla, lemon, orange, pumpkin, chocolate, peppermint—and we sell them individually and in multipacks to devoted fans. So you see, the pop-in-your-mouth, easy-to-make marshmallow was the original catalyst for our side foray into the candy, confection, and chocolate business.

We encourage you not to be scared of candy, confection, and chocolate making. All you need to start is a candy and chocolate thermometer and the willingness to practice. In this chapter, we have provided you with a few simple but wonderfully delicious recipes that will teach you the basics of candy and confection making. The Trio of Truffles (page 169) will introduce you to tempering chocolate, the caramel apples (page 166) are an enjoyable way to learn about caramel, and the marshmallows (page 161) provide a quick and easy lesson on understanding your candy thermometer.

Several of the recipes in this chapter make excellent gifts. Box up the toffee (page 164) with a nice ribbon, pour the sauces (pages 179 and 180) into hand-labeled jars, and pair up your marshmallows with a hot chocolate mix.

VANILLA MARSHMALLOWS

IF YOU HAVE NOT EATEN A HOMEMADE MARSHMALLOW, YOU ARE MISSING OUT ON A RHAPSODIC PLEASURE. It is most certainly not the same marshmallow you know from the grocery store. In fact, it is like comparing a fresh baguette to Wonder Bread. Our recipe produces cloudlike squares that melt in your mouth or in your hot chocolate. They are sticky, sweet, and full of vanilla flavor. Perhaps best of all, they are quite easy to make, and require few ingredients.

YIELD: 48 MARSHMALLOWS

12 sheets gelatin
2 cups sugar
1 cup light corn syrup
2 teaspoons pure vanilla extract

⅛ teaspoon salt
½ cup sifted confectioners' sugar, plus more for dusting

BAKED NOTE

You can flavor your marshmallows with almost any extract or liqueur that suits your needs. Simply replace the vanilla with a few teaspoons of your favorite flavor. Just be aware that some extracts are more powerful than vanilla (like peppermint extract) and won't require the full 2 teaspoons.

Grease a 9-by-13-by-2-inch pan with vegetable shortening: Dab a little bit of shortening on a paper towel and rub it into the sides and bottom of the pan. Set aside.

Put the gelatin sheets in a medium or large heatproof bowl, fill the bowl with very cold water, and set aside; add a few ice cubes to keep the water cold.

In a medium saucepan, gently stir together the sugar, ½ cup of the corn syrup, and ½ cup water. Be careful not to splash the ingredients onto the sides of the pan. Put the saucepan over medium-high heat and clip a candy thermometer to the side of the saucepan.

Fill a medium saucepan halfway with water and place on the stove over medium-low heat.

Put the remaining ½ cup corn syrup in the bowl of an electric mixer fitted with the whisk attachment. Set aside.

Return to the saucepan of water and check the temperature. When the temperature reaches 220 degrees F., drain the water from the bowl of gelatin and give the gelatin sheets a quick wringing out. Place the bowl of gelatin over the saucepan of simmering water and stir the gelatin sheets with a heatproof spatula until the gelatin is completely melted. Remove the bowl from the pan.

Turn the mixer on low speed and slowly pour the melted gelatin into the corn syrup. Keep the mixer on low.

Bring the sugar mixture to the soft ball stage on the candy thermometer (235 to 240 degrees F.), then remove from the heat. Take out the candy thermometer. Turn the mixer up to medium for 1 minute, then slowly pour the sugar mixture into the gelatin mixture. When all of the sugar mixture has been added, turn the mixer to medium-high and beat for about 5 minutes. The marshmallow mixture will begin to turn white and fluffy. Add the vanilla and salt and turn the mixer up to its highest setting for another minute.

Working very quickly, pour the marshmallows into the prepared pan. Use an offset spatula to spread out the mixture evenly. Sprinkle with a bit of sifted confectioners' sugar and let sit for about 6 hours.

Use a knife to loosen the marshmallow from the edges of the pan, and use your hands to pull the marshmallow (it will come out in one gigantic piece) out of the pan and onto a flat surface lightly dusted with confectioners' sugar.

Place the ½ cup confectioners' sugar in a small bowl.

Use a chef's knife to cut the marshmallows into a 6-by-8 grid. Roll each marshmallow in confectioners' sugar. The marshmallows will keep in an airtight container for up to 1 week. Serve with hot chocolate or eat as is.

FRESHLY BAKED IDEA MARSHMALLOW MEN

Use our marshmallow recipe on page 161 to make your own squared-off marshmallow men.
They make adorable place settings and are ideal for holiday gatherings.

STEP 1 First, make one tray of our famous Vanilla Marshmallows.

STEP 2 Cut out eight 2-inch squares (these will be your marshmallow man bottoms) and eight 1-inch squares (these will be your marshmallow man tops) and roll all of the pieces in sifted confectioners' sugar.

STEP 3 Stick a toothpick halfway through each marshmallow man bottom and push the smaller marshmallows down on top of the exposed toothpick until it touches the bottom. You should have eight "snowman"-like marshmallows.

STEP 4 Decorate the marshmallow men however you like. Thin licorice works well for mouths, and mini chocolate chips work great for coal-like eyes. Use sugar glue (recipe follows) for affixing the features.

SIMPLE SUGAR GLUE Put 1 cup sifted confectioners' sugar in a small bowl. Sprinkle 2 tablespoons water over the sugar and whisk until the mixture is cementlike. Keep whisking quickly until the mixture turns from shiny to matte. Add 1 tablespoon more water and whisk again as the mixture begins to harden. Work quickly with the sugar glue to affix mouth, eyes, and nose to your marshmallow men.

PECAN AND ALMOND CHOCOLATE TOFFEE

FOR SOME REASON, WE ONLY MAKE THIS TREAT DURING THE WINTER HOLIDAYS, BUT THERE IS NO REASON IT SHOULDN'T BE MADE ALL YEAR ROUND. This is a simplified version of the classic chocolate toffee, no chocolate tempering required, and it is a truly addictive party treat. You may be tempted to use different nuts, but you should know that the pecan and almond version is the most popular toffee we make. Our toffee makes a great gift. Break it up into 1-ounce pieces and arrange between layers of parchment paper in a gift box or gift tin. If you want to ship your toffee gift, add a substantial layer of bubble wrap to the bottom and top of your box or tin.

YIELD: 1½ POUNDS

1 cup sliced almonds
1 cup toasted pecans
1 cup (2 sticks) unsalted butter, cut
    into 1-inch pieces
1 cup sugar

5 ounces dark chocolate (60 to 72%
    cacao), coarsely chopped
4 ounces milk chocolate,
    coarsely chopped

BAKED NOTE

Timing is everything when making toffee. Make sure you measure out all the ingredients ahead of time, and avoid any distractions (television, phone calls) during the process. You don't want your toffee to burn while it cooks, and you don't want it to cool too much before adding the chocolate and nuts.

Butter a 9-by-13-by-2-inch glass or metal baking pan (do not use nonstick spray).

In the bowl of a food processor, pulse the almonds until they are a fine powder. Place the powdered almonds in a small bowl and set aside. In the same food processor bowl, pulse the pecans for just 1 or 2 seconds, or until they are coarsely chopped but not powdered. Set aside.

Put the butter in a medium pan over low heat. When the butter is halfway melted, add the sugar and 1 tablespoon water and cook over low heat, stirring very gently with a silicone or rubber spatula, until completely combined. Clip a candy thermometer onto the side of the pan, turn the heat up to medium-high, and wait for the mixture to reach 300 degrees F., about 15 minutes. The mixture will start to bubble and turn brown. If the browning seems uneven, swirl the pan during the cooking process but do not stir.

Meanwhile, toss the dark and milk chocolate pieces together.

When the mixture reaches 300 degrees F., remove the pan from the heat and remove the candy thermometer. Stir in the pecan pieces and pour the mixture into the prepared pan. After the mixture has evened out in the pan, wait 1 minute, then sprinkle the chocolate pieces all over the toffee. Wait about 3 minutes for the chocolate to melt, then use an offset spatula to spread the chocolate into an even layer. Sprinkle the almond powder over the melted chocolate, then carefully put the whole pan in the freezer for about 30 minutes.

Remove the pan from the freezer and break the toffee into pieces with a sharp knife. Store the toffee, between layers of parchment, in an airtight container at cool room temperature.

The toffee will keep for up to 5 days.

VANILLA BEAN CARAMEL APPLES

THIS MAY SEEM OBVIOUS, BUT THE SECRET TO A GREAT CARAMEL APPLE IS THE APPLE ITSELF. You should use only the freshest, best-looking, most delicious apples you can find, preferably a tart and crisp variety. At the bakery, we use greenmarket Macouns and Cortlands from upstate New York. These caramel apples are much simpler to make than you might imagine, and they are quite fun to dip. Make a batch, wrap them in cellophane or parchment paper, tie with a bow, and bring them to your next Halloween party.

YIELD: 10–12 APPLES

10 to 12 crisp apples
2 cups heavy cream
1 vanilla bean
2 cups sugar

½ cup light corn syrup
3 tablespoons unsalted butter
Ice

BAKED NOTE

When it comes to dipping the apples in caramel, it is easier to work with small to medium apples. In addition, smaller caramel apples are easier to eat, and the ratio of caramel to apple is just right.

Wash and thoroughly dry the apples. Remove the stems, then set them on parchment-lined baking sheets a few inches apart. Insert a small dowel (about 7 inches long, pencil-sharpened on one end) about three quarters of the way through each apple.

Put the cream in a small heavy pot. Cut the vanilla bean in half lengthwise and, using the tip of the knife or a small teaspoon, scrape the seeds of the vanilla bean into the cream. Add the vanilla bean to the cream.

Simmer the cream and vanilla over very low heat for 10 minutes. Do not let the mixture boil. Remove from the heat and pour the mixture through a fine-mesh sieve into a bowl to remove the vanilla bean and any other fibrous pieces. Vanilla bean flecks will remain.

Return the vanilla cream to the pot, then add the sugar, corn syrup, and butter, making sure that the mixture doesn't splash onto the sides of the pot. Place the pot over very low heat and stir very gently until the sugar is dissolved, to prevent burning. When the sugar is dissolved, increase the heat to medium-high and clip a candy thermometer onto the side of the pot. Heat the caramel mixture, without stirring, to 245 degrees F.

Meanwhile, put a few handfuls of ice in a medium bowl that is large enough to accommodate the pot with the caramel mixture.

When the caramel mixture reaches 245 degrees F. (and stays there for at least 1 minute), remove from the heat and place the pot on top of the ice for 30 seconds to slow the cooking. Remove the pan from the ice.

Tilt the pot toward you to create a big pool of caramel and, working fast, immediately begin dipping the apples in it. Dip each apple only once, and don't worry about coating it evenly or completely (the more you fuss with the caramel the more difficult it will become to dip). Return the caramel-dipped apples back to the baking sheet and refrigerate until the caramel is set, about 10 minutes. Serve.

MAPLE CARAMEL APPLES

Omit the vanilla bean and add 1½ tablespoons pure maple extract. Obviously, you do not have to steep the maple extract. Just combine the cream, sugar, corn syrup, butter, and maple extract in the pot, heat the mixture to 245 degrees F., and continue with the recipe.

A TRIO OF TRUFFLES

WHY MAKE JUST ONE TRUFFLE FLAVOR WHEN YOU CAN MAKE THREE? We couldn't decide which truffle flavor we wanted to be part of the book, so we decided to include our top three. Each of these truffles has a snappy chocolate exterior and a melt-in-your-mouth ganache center. With a little chocolate tempering skill, you can make these truffles quite easily and impress your friends and family with a great homemade holiday gift.

YIELD: 18 TRUFFLES

HONEY AND DARK CHOCOLATE TRUFFLES

FOR THE TRUFFLE CENTER

9 ounces dark chocolate (60 to 72% cacao), coarsely chopped
1 cup heavy cream
¼ cup honey
1 teaspoon espresso powder

FOR THE TRUFFLE COATING

¼ cup confectioners' sugar, sifted
Tempered Dark Chocolate (see page 173)

BAKED NOTE

Tempered chocolate gives truffles a glossy shine and an exterior with a classic chocolate "snap"; nontempered chocolate will look dull, almost grayish, and the chocolate will be soft to the bite.

MAKE THE TRUFFLE CENTERS

Place the chocolate in a large heatproof bowl. Place a fine-mesh sieve or strainer over the bowl and set aside.

In a medium-sized, heavy-bottomed saucepan, stir together the cream, honey, and espresso powder. Heat the mixture just to a boil.

Remove the saucepan from the heat, and pour the cream mixture through the sieve directly over the chocolate. Let the cream sit for 2 minutes. Gently stir the mixture from the center outward until it is smooth and shiny. Cover the entire bowl in plastic wrap, making sure the chocolate surface comes in direct contact with the plastic wrap. Refrigerate for 5 hours or until firm.

Line a baking sheet with parchment paper.

Scoop the truffles with a small melon baller or tablespoon, and drop onto the parchment paper in balls (balls will not be perfectly round). Place the baking sheet in the freezer for 20 minutes.

ROLLING THE TRUFFLES

Spread out the confectioners' sugar on a small plate. Remove the truffles from the freezer and use a dipping fork or fondue fork to dip each truffle in the tempered chocolate (or use your fingers), then drop the truffle in the sugar and roll to coat. Put the sugar-coated truffles on the baking sheet to set.

Truffles can be stored in an airtight container, between layers of wax or parchment paper, in the refrigerator for up to 1 week.

MILK CHOCOLATE ALMOND TRUFFLES

FOR THE TRUFFLE CENTERS

8 ounces milk chocolate, coarsely chopped
¾ cup heavy cream
¼ cup sliced almonds, toasted
1 teaspoon almond extract or 1 teaspoon
   Amaretto liqueur

FOR THE TRUFFLE COATING

¼ cup sliced almonds, toasted and
   coarsely chopped
Tempered Milk Chocolate (see page 173)

MAKE THE TRUFFLE CENTERS

Place the chocolate in a large heatproof bowl. Place a fine-mesh sieve or strainer over the bowl and set aside.

In a medium-sized, heavy-bottomed saucepan, heat the cream just to a boil. Add the almonds, cover the saucepan, and turn the heat down to simmer. Simmer the almonds in the covered saucepan for 20 minutes.

Remove the saucepan from the heat, and pour the cream through the sieve directly over the chocolate. Let the mixture sit for 2 minutes. Gently stir the mixture from the center outward until it is smooth and shiny. Add the almond extract or liqueur and stir to combine. Cover the entire bowl in plastic wrap, making sure the chocolate surface comes in direct contact with the plastic wrap. Refrigerate for 5 hours or until firm.

Line a baking sheet with parchment paper.

Scoop the truffles with a small melon baller or tablespoon, and drop onto parchment paper in balls (balls will not be perfectly round). Place the baking sheet in the freezer for 20 minutes.

ROLLING THE TRUFFLES

Place the almonds on a large plate.

Remove the truffles from the freezer and use a dipping fork or fondue fork to dip each truffle in the tempered chocolate (or use your fingers), then drop the truffle in the almonds and turn to coat with almond pieces. Put the almond-coated truffles on the baking sheet to set.

Truffles can be stored in an airtight container, between layers of wax or parchment paper, for up to 1 week.

CHOCOLATE RASPBERRY TRUFFLES

FOR THE TRUFFLE CENTERS

1½ cups frozen raspberries

9 ounces dark chocolate (60 to 72% cacao), coarsely chopped

¾ cup heavy cream

1 tablespoon honey

2 tablespoons unsalted butter, softened

FOR THE TRUFFLE COATING

¼ cup red sanding sugar

Tempered Dark Chocolate (see page 173)

MAKE THE RASPBERRY PUREE

In a small saucepan over low heat, warm the raspberries to soften, then push the raspberries through a fine-mesh sieve or strainer into a small bowl. Discard the raspberry seeds.

MAKE THE TRUFFLE CENTERS

Place the chocolate in a large heatproof bowl. Place a fine-mesh sieve or strainer over the bowl and set aside.

In a medium-sized, heavy-bottomed saucepan, stir together the cream, honey, and raspberry puree. Heat the mixture just to a boil.

Remove the saucepan from the heat, and pour the cream mixture through the sieve directly over the chocolate. Let the mixture sit for 2 minutes. Gently stir the mixture from the center outward until it is smooth and shiny. Add the butter and stir until combined. Cover the entire bowl in plastic wrap, making sure the chocolate surface comes in direct contact with the plastic wrap. Refrigerate for 5 hours or until firm.

Line a baking sheet with parchment.

Scoop the truffles with a small melon baller or tablespoon, and drop onto the parchment paper in balls (balls will not be perfectly round). Place the baking sheet in the freezer for 20 minutes.

ROLLING THE TRUFFLES

Spread out the sanding sugar on a small plate.

Remove the truffles from the freezer and use a dipping fork or fondue fork to dip each truffle in the tempered chocolate (or use your fingers), then drop the truffle in the sugar and roll to coat. Put the sugar-coated truffles on the baking sheet to set.

Truffles can be stored in an airtight container, between layers of wax or parchment paper, in the refrigerator for up to 1 week.

HOW TO TEMPER CHOCOLATE

There are many methods of tempering chocolate, but each is accomplished through a process of melting, cooling, and agitating. Our favorite method is to seed the chocolate. Here, a portion of already tempered chocolate is added to melted chocolate. This helps stimulate the formation of stable beta crystals—or, to put it simply, reduces the temperature of the melted chocolate and helps it come to temper.

Before you start, keep in mind it is best to temper chocolate in a cool kitchen. Measure out 1 pound of chocolate — dark or milk, depending on the recipe — and chop well with a serrated knife. We prefer to use a couverture chocolate that contains at least 32% cocoa butter, as it is thinner when melted and ideal for dipping.

Reserve about a quarter of this chocolate. Put the remainder in a large heatproof bowl and place over a pot of simmering water. Melt the chocolate until an instant-read thermometer placed in the middle of the bowl reads 120 degrees F.

Remove the bowl from the heat and add the reserved chopped chocolate. With a rubber spatula, stir the chocolate vigorously without stopping until it has completely melted and cooled to a temperature of 80 degrees F. The chocolate should thicken considerably.

Place the bowl of chocolate back over the simmering water and stir with a spatula. If you are using dark chocolate, bring it to a temperature between 86 and 90 degrees F. If you are using milk chocolate, a temperature between 84 and 87 degrees F. works best.

Test the chocolate to make sure it has reached a full temper. Dip a small metal spatula into the chocolate and place it on the counter. The chocolate should begin to set in 3–5 minutes and have a satiny shine, without streaks. If the chocolate has not set after 5 minutes or it looks speckled or streaked, you should continue to agitate the chocolate with the spatula until it is properly tempered.

When your chocolate is tempered, you may begin dipping. Keep in mind that tempered chocolate sets up quickly. If you notice the chocolate in your bowl is beginning to harden, place it back over the simmering water to reheat, but only for a few seconds.

BANANA PECAN PILONCILLO ICE CREAM

MOVE OVER, BANANA BREAD. This is the best way to use up any leftover or forgotten ripe bananas hiding in your kitchen. Light in texture and not overly rich, this ice cream was discovered by Matt on a trip to Oaxaca, Mexico. Piloncillo is an unrefined Mexican cane sugar that gives this ice cream a slightly musky molasses flavor. Matt has since become a piloncillo advocate.

YIELD: ABOUT 1 QUART

1 cinnamon stick
¾ cup firmly packed, grated piloncillo
8 very ripe bananas, peeled, wrapped in
   aluminum foil, and frozen

½ cup heavy cream
½ cup finely chopped toasted pecans

BAKED NOTE

Piloncillo is available in Latin American supermarkets and specialty grocery stores. If you have trouble finding it, you can substitute dark brown sugar or muscovado sugar, but we highly recommend you use piloncillo, as it has a really unique flavor.

In a small saucepan over low heat, combine 2 tablespoons plus 1 teaspoon water and the cinnamon stick and simmer until fragrant, about 3 minutes. Add the piloncillo and stir until it is dissolved. Remove from the heat and let cool to room temperature.

Unwrap the frozen bananas, chop them coarsely, and set them aside.

Remove the cinnamon stick from the syrup and pour the syrup into a blender. Add the cream and bananas and blend until smooth and mushy.

Pour into an ice cream machine and freeze, following the manufacturer's directions. Add the pecans to the ice cream a few minutes before the cycle is finished, or consult the manufacturer's directions about additions. Since the mixture is partially frozen, it will not take long to freeze—about 10 minutes.

MOCHA FUDGESICLES

OUR MOCHA FUDGESICLES ARE ESSENTIALLY CHOCOLATE PUDDING POPS. The ingredients and directions are very similar to those for making a simple, delicious homemade pudding, but we decided to pour the pudding mixture into ice pop molds for a quick and easy frozen treat perfect for picnics, pool parties, and late-night movies. Flavors lose their intensity when frozen, so you may want to increase the amount of instant espresso powder in this recipe if you want a more pronounced coffee flavor.

YIELD: 8–10 POPS

BAKED NOTE

You don't have to use ice pop molds. For bite-sized snacks, pour the mixture into ice cube trays, cover the tray tightly with plastic wrap, and insert toothpicks three quarters of the way down into the liquid. Freeze and serve.

1 tablespoon unsalted butter
½ cup sugar
2 tablespoons dark unsweetened cocoa powder
1 tablespoon instant espresso powder
2 tablespoons all-purpose flour
2 tablespoons cornstarch
1 large egg
¼ cup heavy cream
2¾ cups whole milk

Put the butter in a large heatproof bowl and set aside.

In a large saucepan, whisk together the sugar, cocoa powder, instant espresso powder, flour, and cornstarch. Add the egg and cream and whisk until combined.

Place the saucepan over medium heat and slowly pour in the milk, whisking constantly. Increase the heat to medium-high and bring to a boil, whisking occasionally. After the mixture boils, continue to cook, whisking, for another 2 minutes.

Remove from the heat and pour the mixture over the butter. Whisk vigorously for 1 minute to cool slightly. Let the mixture cool for 15 minutes, whisk vigorously for 1 minute, then pour into ice pop molds. Freeze until hard, about 6 hours. Release the pops from the mold by quickly running some hot water along the plastic surface of the mold (be sure not to let the water touch the pops), then pull the pops out of the mold.

DARK CHOCOLATE ICE CREAM

DEEPER AND DARKER AND RICHER THAN ANY STORE-BOUGHT VERSION, OUR DARK CHOCOLATE ICE CREAM IS INSANELY ADDICTIVE. We originally made this ice cream with the black cocoa powder from King Arthur Flour, but it was just too intense (good, but intense). If you happen to come across their black cocoa (and it is well worth having some around the kitchen), use 1 tablespoon black cocoa powder and 3 tablespoons regular unsweetened cocoa powder. This tempers the intensity of the flavor.

YIELD: ABOUT 1½ QUARTS

8 ounces dark chocolate (60 to 72% cacao), finely chopped
4 large eggs
1½ cups heavy cream

1 cup milk
¾ cup sugar
¼ cup dark unsweetened cocoa powder

BAKED NOTE

This ice cream is regal on its own, but if you are going to use a mix-in we suggest salted pretzels, broken up into tiny bits. Mix-ins are typically added a few minutes before the ice cream is finished freezing in the ice cream machine, but follow the manufacturer's instruction manual for exact timing.

Put the chocolate in the bowl of an electric mixer. Set aside.

In a large bowl, beat the eggs until just combined.

Combine the cream, milk, sugar, and cocoa powder in a small saucepan and bring just to a boil. Remove from the heat and pour one third of the mixture into the eggs, whisking constantly. Add another third of the mixture and whisk again. Return the egg mixture to the saucepan over medium heat. Whisking constantly, bring to 170 degrees F. on a chocolate thermometer. Remove from the heat and pour through a fine-mesh sieve directly into the chocolate. Let the mixture sit for 1 minute, then slowly whisk until combined.

Put the mixture in the refrigerator for 4 hours (or overnight), then whisk until the mixture is thick and frothy. Pour into an ice cream machine and freeze, following the manufacturer's instructions, until the mixture looks like a very firm pudding. Put in an airtight container and freeze for at least 6 hours, or until hard.

BROWN SUGAR CARAMEL SAUCE

YOU WILL WANT TO DRINK THIS SAUCE. It is absolutely delicious, and we find ourselves looking for things to pour it over as an excuse to use it. Obviously, it's amazing over ice cream, cakes, and cheesecake, but feel free to use it however you please (and don't be embarrassed if you find yourself just eating it straight from the jar with a spoon).

YIELD: 1½ CUPS

¾ cup firmly packed light brown sugar
¼ cup light corn syrup
¾ cup heavy cream

1 teaspoon pure vanilla extract
Small pinch fleur de sel (optional)

BAKED NOTE

Homemade caramel sauce is delicious and easy, but a tad messy. Instead of trying to scrub caramel out of the pan, just put any caramel-covered utensils (including the bottom of your thermometer) in the pan you used to cook the caramel. Fill the pan halfway with water and bring to a boil. The caramel will melt away, and your pan and utensils will wipe clean.

In a medium saucepan with high sides, stir the brown sugar, ½ cup water, and the corn syrup together. Stir gently so you don't splash any of the mixture onto the sides of the pan. Cook over medium-high heat, stirring until the sugar dissolves. Increase the heat to high and stop stirring. The mixture will begin to boil. Boil for 10 minutes. Remove from the heat and slowly add the cream, whisking gently. The caramel will bubble vigorously when the cream is added, and will then clump.

Return the pan to low heat and warm the mixture to dissolve the caramel clumps. When the caramel is smooth, add the vanilla and salt, if using, and whisk again.

If using the sauce immediately, remove from the heat and beat vigorously to cool it slightly. Let stand for a few minutes before pouring over ice cream or cake.

Let any leftover caramel sauce come to room temperature, cover, and refrigerate. You can rewarm the sauce in a microwave oven or in a double boiler. The caramel will keep in a tightly sealed jar in the refrigerator for up to 5 days.

MALTED MILK CHOCOLATE SAUCE

THIS IS A RIFF ON THE CLASSIC THICK HOT FUDGE SAUCE FOUND IN NUMEROUS SODA FOUNTAINS AND ICE CREAM SHOPS THROUGHOUT THE UNITED STATES. We added a touch of chocolate malt powder for old-fashioned toasty flavor and made the traditionally dark chocolate sauce with a handful of good-quality milk chocolate. What results is a well-balanced, smooth, rich sauce that is perfect for topping ice cream, pies, and pound cake.

YIELD: 2 CUPS

BAKED NOTE

Give the gift of malt. Double this recipe, let it cool completely, and pour it into 8 4-ounce jars. Personalize the jars with a decorative label and be sure to include heating instructions.

 MALTED MILK SHAKE

⅔ cup heavy cream
⅓ cup light corn syrup
¼ cup chocolate malt Ovaltine
¼ cup firmly packed light brown sugar
½ teaspoon salt

6 ounces good-quality milk chocolate, coarsely chopped
2 tablespoons unsalted butter
1 teaspoon pure vanilla extract

In a large saucepan, bring the cream, corn syrup, Ovaltine, brown sugar, salt, and 4 ounces of the chocolate to a boil over medium heat. Stir until smooth and the chocolate has melted. Reduce the heat to maintain a simmer and, stirring very slowly, cook for 5 minutes.

Remove from the heat and stir in the butter, vanilla, and the remaining 2 ounces chocolate. Let the sauce cool for 5 to 10 minutes before serving.

To store, cool the sauce completely and refrigerate in an airtight container for up to 5 days. Reheat in a microwave oven or over low heat on the stovetop.

2 large scoops ice cream
2 tablespoons Malted Milk
  Chocolate Sauce
½ cup whole milk

Our Malted Milk Chocolate Sauce can also be used to make a terrific milk shake: Blend together the ice cream, Malted Milk Chocolate Sauce, and milk until smooth. Pour the milkshake into a chilled glass and drizzle one more spoonful of the sauce on top before serving.

We suppose we should extend our diet beyond cake and cocktails, but we can't think of many good reasons why. In our humble opinion, a great after-dinner drink should satisfy like a great dessert, only with more alcohol. Of course, not every recipe in this chapter contains alcohol, and a few, like the Adult Hot Chocolate (page 191), taste just as delicious without it.

The drink recipes compiled in this chapter all have a sweet profile, as befitting a book by the owners of a bakery. Chocolate, ice cream, and fruit are interspersed with coffee, spirits, and teas to create our favorite dessert drinks or drink desserts. The more obvious dessert-style drinks, like the Vanilla Bean Affogato (page 185), the Chocolate Stout Milkshake (page 188), and the Baked Brown Cow (page 187), can be served in place of a typical dessert, while the lighter drinks can be served "cocktail style" at the beginning of or during a meal.

The beauty of these recipes is that they are decidedly more forgiving than baking recipes. They are less scientific. You can increase or decrease the amount of matcha powder to taste in our Green Tea Smoothie (page 192), for example, and the drink will still be a smoothie, and it will still taste delicious. Don't hesitate to take liberties with these recipes to create your own.

Also, all of these recipes can easily be doubled, tripled, or quintupled for large gatherings. Since most of our drink recipes are on the sweet side, small four-ounce servings are ideal for most soirées.

Our final bit of advice regarding drinks: Make sure you serve them in the correct glass or drinkware. We are not snobs, but our Chocolate Stout Milkshake looks so much more appetizing in a tall, chilled glass than it would in a plastic tumbler or coffee mug. The same goes for our Espresso Martini (page 186): Use a martini glass! It is very sad to see a martini served in an ordinary water glass.

We hope you enjoy these recipes. They have kept us very happy over the years.

VANILLA BEAN AFFOGATO

HOT COFFEE, COLD ICE CREAM: THIS IS TRULY A DESSERT THAT EVERYONE CAN MAKE. *Affogare* is Italian for "to drown," which is just what the espresso does to the ice cream here. If you're like us, you may want to wait a few minutes for the ice cream to melt into the hot espresso a little and pool in the bottom of the glass. Make sure to capture a bit of still-cold ice cream in each spoonful.

YIELD: 4 SERVINGS

1 pint premium vanilla ice cream
1 vanilla bean
½ cup freshly brewed hot espresso

BAKED NOTE

Freshly brewed espresso is hard to substitute, but if you don't have access to an espresso machine, dissolve a few tablespoons of instant espresso powder in ½ cup boiling water.

Divide the ice cream among 4 wide-mouth tumblers or serving bowls. Put the tumblers in the freezer while you prep your espresso.

Cut the vanilla bean in half lengthwise and, using the tip of the knife or a small teaspoon, scrape the seeds of the vanilla bean into the hot espresso. Stir gently.

Slowly pour the espresso mixture over the ice cream in the tumblers. Serve immediately, with small spoons.

ESPRESSO MARTINI

RENATO KNOWS A THING OR TWO ABOUT THE ESPRESSO MARTINI. It can be a fabulous after-dinner drink or a watery, sugary mess. This recipe is the perfect distillation of what Renato feels an espresso martini should be. On occasion, for casual dinner parties, we will serve Espresso Martinis with a plate of very dark chocolate cut into small bites in lieu of a traditional plated dessert. It's light, festive, and the perfect way to end an evening (or start one).

YIELD: 2 MARTINIS

BAKED NOTE

For a garnish, pour a shallow layer of cocoa powder onto a plate that is wider than the rim of the martini glass. Wet the rim of the chilled glass with a slice of lemon and dip the rim into the cocoa powder. Lift the glass from the cocoa and lightly tap it to remove the excess powder.

2 espresso beans
2 ounces (2 shots) room-temperature or slightly cold freshly brewed espresso
4 ounces vanilla-flavored vodka
2 ounces coffee-flavored liqueur (such as Kahlúa)

Put two martini glasses in the freezer to chill for up to 1 hour.

Put one espresso bean in the bottom of each glass.

Pour the espresso, vodka, and coffee liqueur into a shaker filled with ice and shake vigorously. Strain into the glasses and serve immediately.

BAKED BROWN COW

A BROWN COW HAS MANY DEFINITIONS. Some people insist it is akin to a root beer float, while others say it's a cream-filled cocktail. We decided to take some liberties and created our own version, the Baked Brown Cow. This is like an ice cream sundae for adults. Rich-tasting, yet simple to make, and with that final dusting of nutmeg, it can be the playful ending to a wonderful dinner.

YIELD: 2 SERVINGS

BAKED NOTE

You can use any liqueur in place of the Kahlúa. You can make an orange cow with Grand Marnier or a red cow (raspberry-flavored) with Chambord, for example.

3 ounces dark chocolate (60 to 72% cacao), coarsely chopped

¼ cup plus 1 tablespoon heavy cream

2 huge scoops (about 2 cups) premium vanilla ice cream

2 shots coffee-flavored liqueur (such as Kahlúa)

Freshly grated nutmeg

Put the chocolate in a small heatproof bowl. In a small pot, bring the cream just to a boil. Immediately pour it over the chocolate. Let the mixture stand for 1 minute, then stir until smooth. Spoon about 2 tablespoons of the chocolate mixture into the bottom of an old fashioned glass. Using the back of the spoon, spread the sauce evenly in the bottom and slightly up the sides of the glass.

Divide the ice cream between the glasses and let stand for about 5 minutes to melt slightly. Pour one shot of Kahlúa over each serving and garnish with a dusting of nutmeg. Serve immediately, with big ol' spoons.

FRESHLY BAKED IDEA GIVE GLASS

It is always acceptable to give a bottle of wine or Champagne to the host or hostess of a party, but why not give them something to drink it out of instead? Many times, we have walked into a party and handed over a bottle of delicious wine, and the host thanked us and placed it next to the other thirty-five bottles he or she received that night. Though the wine will eventually be drunk and enjoyed, we can guarantee that the host would be grateful for a new set of drinkware. As many party hosts know, glasses break quite often when the festivities reach a boozy pitch. A simple pair of basic wine, martini, or other barware glasses will always be appreciated.

CHOCOLATE STOUT MILKSHAKE

THIS DRINK COMBINES TWO OF OUR FAVORITE THINGS: CHOCOLATE ICE CREAM AND ICE-COLD STOUT. Though not a common combination, they taste wonderful together. (Actually, this pairing deserves a more thorough analysis, as it is downright harmonious.) The creamy malt stout brings out a robustness in the ice cream that is magical. We highly recommend that you use a chocolate stout for this drink. Many microbreweries produce versions we like, such as Young's Chocolate Stout or Brooklyn Brewery's Black Chocolate Stout. As much as we like Guinness and other dry stouts, they are too light and dry for this concoction.

YIELD: 2 (8-OUNCE) SERVINGS

BAKED NOTE

This recipe is a perfect party drink and works great in smaller, four-ounce servings as a passed refreshment.

2 huge scoops (about 2 cups) premium
   chocolate ice cream
½ cup whole milk
¼ cup very cold chocolate stout
1 tablespoon malted milk powder

Put two tall (8-ounce or larger), heavy glasses in the freezer while you make the milkshake.

Put the ice cream, milk, stout, and malted milk powder in a powerful blender. Blend until smooth. Pour into the chilled glasses and serve with spoons.

CINNAMON MOCHA

A CLASSIC MOCHA IS ALL WELL AND GOOD, BUT OUR ADDITION OF CINNAMON GIVES IT A WELCOME WARMTH. Depending on your personality, this is either a coffee drink or a hot chocolate drink, but either way it is an extraordinary wintry treat and one of Renato's favorites. The addition of whipped cream is pure indulgence, a perfect example of our drink-as-dessert philosophy.

YIELD: 2 (8-OUNCE) SERVINGS

BAKED NOTE

You can replace the espresso in this recipe with double-strength coffee. Use twice the recommended amount of ground coffee when you brew it.

¼ cup plus 2 tablespoons dark unsweetened cocoa powder

¼ cup sugar

1 teaspoon cinnamon, plus more for garnish

2 long shots freshly brewed espresso

2 cups whole milk

Simple Vanilla Bean Whipped Cream (page 103), optional

In a small heatproof bowl, whisk together the cocoa powder, sugar, and cinnamon. Slowly add the hot espresso and whisk until the mixture is smooth.

In a medium saucepan, heat the milk over medium heat. Add the espresso mixture and whisk until combined. Stirring constantly, bring the mixture to a boil, then remove from the heat.

Divide the mocha evenly between two mugs and top with whipped cream, if desired, and a dash of cinnamon. Serve immediately with a small spoon.

ADULT HOT CHOCOLATE

THIS HOT CHOCOLATE RECIPE IS A DESSERT UNTO ITSELF. Add marshmallows or whipped cream, and enjoy this rich, smooth, and chocolatey chocolate in front of a roaring fire. You can make it in a matter of minutes, and it tastes infinitely better than the instant powdered stuff.

YIELD: 2 SERVINGS

BAKED NOTE

This recipe makes a very rich, semi-thick hot chocolate. To make a lighter version, simply replace the whole milk with low-fat or skim milk.

2 ounces good-quality milk chocolate, coarsely chopped

5 ounces good-quality dark chocolate (60 to 72% cacao), coarsely chopped

½ cup boiling water

¾ cup whole milk

¼ cup heavy cream

1 tablespoon maple syrup

2 tablespoons amaretto liqueur

Simple Vanilla Bean Whipped Cream (page 103), optional

Crushed amaretti cookies, optional

Put the chocolates in a small heatproof bowl.

Pour the boiling water over the chocolate, and make sure most of the chocolate is submerged. Let the chocolate sit for 1 minute, then whisk until smooth. Set aside.

In a small saucepan over low heat, bring the milk, cream, and maple syrup just to a simmer. Pour the chocolate mixture into the milk mixture and whisk until combined. Turn the heat up to medium and cook, whisking constantly, until the mixture is just about to boil. Add the amaretto, stir one more time, and ladle into two mugs. Top with whipped cream and crushed amaretti cookies, if desired, and serve immediately.

GREEN TEA SMOOTHIE

MATCHA POWDER, OR POWDERED GREEN TEA, HAS A UNIQUE TASTE. We've heard it described as sweetly vegetal and earthy, but these descriptions don't really pinpoint the distinctive taste of matcha. The best way to try it is in our Green Tea Smoothie. It is completely refreshing, relatively healthful, and tastes damn good on a hot summer day. Matcha powder is an acquired taste for some. If you're a beginning matcha drinker, you may want to start with 1 to 2 teaspoons, then taste and add more matcha as desired.

YIELD: 2 (8-OUNCE) SERVINGS

2 huge scoops (about 2 cups) premium
    vanilla frozen yogurt
½ cup plain soy milk
½ cup chopped honeydew melon
1 tablespoon unsweetened matcha
    powder

BAKED NOTE

For a more indulgent matcha milkshake, swap the soy milk with whole milk and the frozen yogurt with vanilla ice cream. After blending, top with whipped cream and a drizzle of honey.

Put the yogurt, soy milk, honeydew melon, and matcha powder in a powerful blender. Blend until smooth. Pour into two chilled glasses and serve immediately.

ALMOND GRANITA

THIS RECIPE WAS BORN OF A DEEPLY ROOTED FOOD MEMORY. This is the drink that Renato remembers from his childhood summers spent in Sicily. The almond granita of his youth—icy, nutty, almost milky, and scented with a hint of cinnamon—provided sweet relief from the hot African sirocco winds, and it was usually served at breakfast with a sweet brioche. Our almond granita is an adaptation of the one Renato's mother used to serve, and it is just as thirst quenching on a hot summer day.

YIELD: 1 QUART

1 cup blanched almonds
½ cup sugar
½ teaspoon pure almond extract
¼ teaspoon cinnamon
1¼ cups hot water
3 cups cold water

BAKED NOTE

For a nuttier taste and texture, use ¼ cup toasted and cooled almonds and ¾ cup blanched almonds.

Put the almonds, sugar, almond extract, and cinnamon in a food processor and pulse until very finely ground, about 5 minutes, stopping to scrape down the bowl every minute or so.

Slowly pour ¼ cup hot water in through the lid and process until the mixture is a fine paste.

Add another cup hot water in the same way. The mixture will lighten in color slightly and become a concentrated almond "milk."

Transfer the mixture to a 9-by-13-inch glass baking pan. Add cold water and stir to combine. Cover with aluminum foil and put in the freezer for 1 hour.

After 1 hour, uncover the pan and scrape the edges of the granita with a fork, stirring the ice pieces into the center, then cover again and return to the freezer until solid, scraping and stirring every 30 to 45 minutes. When the granita is frozen solid, scrape the surface with a fork and scoop it into serving glasses. Serve immediately.

The granita will keep in the freezer in an airtight container for up to 4 days.

ICED RASPBERRY TEA GRANITA

OUR ICED RASPBERRY TEA GRANITA IS THE ANTIDOTE TO MUGGY, SWELTERING SUMMER HEAT. Serve these icy concoctions in small but classy glasses with a demitasse spoon and make a big splash at your next brunch. It's got the taste of a Champagne spritzer and the texture of a snow cone.

YIELD: ABOUT 4 SERVINGS

½ pound raspberries (about ¾ cup)
½ pound strawberries (about ¾ cup)
⅔ cup sugar
1 cup raspberry iced tea (or other fruit tea)
¾ cup Champagne
Grated zest of 1 lime
Handful of fresh raspberries for garnish

BAKED NOTE

Avoid fruit substitutions in this recipe, as different fruits contain vastly different amounts of water, which can affect the texture and freezing time of the granita.

In the bowl of a food processor, pulse the raspberries, strawberries, and sugar together until smooth. Add the iced tea, Champagne, and lime zest and pulse until combined.

Pour the mixture through a fine-mesh sieve directly into an 8-inch square metal baking pan, cover tightly with aluminum foil, and put in the freezer. Use a fork to scrape or stir the mixture every hour for about 6 hours, or until the granita is frozen.

Use the tines of the fork to scrape the granita, creating flakes. Divide the flakes evenly among 4 glasses, garnish each with a single raspberry, and serve with small spoons.

APPENDIX

SOURCES

CANDY

Economy Candy
108 Rivington Street
New York, NY 10022
800.325.0026
www.economycandy.com

Red Hots (Cinnamon Imperials) and a
multitude of other candies and chocolates.

Koppers Chocolate
800.325.0026
www.kopperschocolate.com

Malted milk balls (Whoppers), lemon
pearls (Lemonheads), Orange Milkies
(chocolate candies) available in bulk
quantitites.

M&M's
800.627.7852
www.m-ms.com

You can get M&M's pretty much anywhere
but if you would like custom colors, you
can order them online.

CHOCOLATE

Callebaut Chocolate
www.callebaut.com

Jacques Torres
350 Hudson Street
New York, NY 10014
212.414.2462
www.mrchocolate.com

Scharffen Berger
914 Heinz Avenue
Berkeley, CA 94710
800.930.4528
www.scharffenberger.com

Valrhona Chocolate
www.lepicerie.com

KITCHEN & BAKING EQUIPMENT

Crate & Barrel
Call 800.967.6696 for store
locations in your area.
www.crateandbarrel.com

JB Prince
800.473.0577
www.jbprince.com

**King Arthur Flour Bakers
Catalogue**
135 Route 5 South
Norwich, VT 05005
800.827.6836
www.kingarthurflour.com

Kitchen Aid Appliances
Call 800.334.6889 for a Kitchen
Aid distributor in your area.
www.kitchenaid.com

New York Cake & Bake
56 West 22nd Street
New York, NY 10010
800.942.2539
www.nycake.com

A fantastic resource for the New York–
based baker. Pans, tools, and decorating
equipment.

Pfeil & Holing
58-15 Northern Boulevard
Woodside, NY 11377
800.247.7955
www.cakedeco.com

Decorating supplies sold in bulk.

Sur La Table

Call 800.243.0852 for store locations in your area.
www.surlatable.com

Williams-Sonoma

Call 800.541.1262 for store locations in your area.
www.williams-sonoma.com

Matcha Source

877.9MATCHA
www.matchasource.com

Matcha powder and assorted teas.

Special Fortune Cookies

3777 Stevens Creek Boulevard
Suite 250
Santa Clara, CA 95051
408.236.6680
www.specialfortunecookies.com

An online resource for custom and special fortune cookies.

Whole Foods

www.wholefoodsmarkets.com

Organic foods as well as a great variety of high-grade chocolates. for locations in your area.

Gourmet Sleuth

PO Box 508
Los Gatos, CA 95031
408.354.8281
www.gourmetsleuth.com

We found chipotle powder, gelatin sheets, piloncillo (panela), instant espresso powder, and other great items on this site.

CONVERSION CHART

Weight Equivalents: The metric weights given in this chart are not exact equivalents, but have been rounded up or down slightly to make measuring easier.

Volume Equivalents: These are not exact equivalents for American cups and spoons, but have been rounded up or down slightly to make measuring easier.

AVOIRDUPOIS	METRIC
1/4 oz	7 g
1/2 oz	15 g
1 oz	30 g
2 oz	60 g
3 oz	90 g
4 oz	115 g
5 oz	150 g
6 oz	175 g
7 oz	200 g
8 oz (1/2 lb)	225 g
9 oz	250 g
10 oz	300 g
11 oz	325 g
12 oz	350 g
13 oz	375 g
14 oz	400 g
15 oz	425 g
16 oz (1 lb)	450 g
1 1/2 lb	750 g
2 lb	900 g
2 1/4 lb	1 kg
3 lb	1.4 kg
4 lb	1.8 kg

AMERICAN	METRIC	IMPERIAL
1/4 tsp	1.2 ml	
1/2 tsp	2.5 ml	
1 tsp	5.0 ml	
½ Tbsp (1.5 tsp)	7.5 ml	
1 Tbsp (3 tsp)	15 ml	
1/4 cup (4 Tbsp)	60 ml	2 fl oz
1/3 cup (5 Tbsp)	75 ml	2.5 fl oz
1/2 cup (8 Tbsp)	125 ml	4 fl oz
2/3 cup (10 Tbsp)	150 ml	5 fl oz
3/4 cup (12 Tbsp)	175 ml	6 fl oz
1 cup (16 Tbsp)	250 ml	8 fl oz
1 1/4 cups	300 ml	10 fl oz (½ pint)
1½ cups	350 ml	12 fl oz
2 cups (1 pint)	500 ml	16 fl oz
2½ cups	625 ml	20 fl oz (1 pint)
1 quart	1 liter	32 fl oz

OVEN MARK	F	C	GAS
Very cool	250–275	130–140	1/2–1
Cool	300	150	2
Warm	325	170	3
Moderate	350	180	4
Moderately hot	375	190	5
	400	200	6
Hot	425	220	7
	450	230	8
Very hot	475	250	9

INDEX

W

walnut
    baked bar filling, 122–23
    maple scones, 29–30
    oatmeal cherry cookies, 146
    tollhouse pie, 98–99
whipped cream, 81
    vanilla bean, 103
whisk, 20
white cake, 55–56, 60
white chocolate
    baked bar filling, 122–23
    Black Forest cookies, 142–43
    fortune cookies dipped in, 79
    frosting, 55–56
whoopie pies, 151–52
Whoppers, 60, 129

Z

zesting, 18, 41

RECIPE INDEX

Published in 2008 by Stewart, Tabori & Chang
An imprint of Harry N. Abrams, Inc.

Library of Congress Cataloging-in-Publication Data

Lewis, Matt.
  Baked : new frontiers in baking / by Matt Lewis and Renato Poliafito.
    p. cm.
  ISBN 978-1-58479-721-0
  1. Baking. 2. Desserts. 3. Baked (Bakery) I. Poliafito, Renato. II.
Title.
  TX765.L67 2008
  641.8'15--dc22
                          2008007814

Editor: Luisa Weiss
Designer: Alissa Faden
Production Manager: Tina Cameron

The text of this book was composed in Eureka,
Akzidenz Grotesk, Rosewood, and Ironmonger.

Printed and bound in China
10 9 8 7 6 5 4 3 2 1

HNA

harry n. abrams, inc.
a subsidiary of La Martinière Groupe
115 West 18th Street
New York, NY 10011
www.hnabooks.com